Scarlett Johansson

Scarlett Johansson

The Illustrated Biography

Chris Roberts

CARLTON
BOOKS

THIS IS A CARLTON BOOK

Published in 2007 by Carlton Books Ltd.
20 Mortimer Street
London W1T 3JW

ISBN: 978-1-84442-399-6

A catalogue record of this book is
available from the British Library.

Editor: **Lara Maiklem**

Art Director: **Lucy Coley**

Design: **Barbara Zuñiga**

Production: **Janette Burgin**

Printed and bound in Dubai
10 9 8 7 6 5 4 3 2 1

Contents

Introduction

Scarlett Marie Johansson is already at the top of her profession, and one of the most famous, fêted, instantly recognizable young women in the world.

"Do I ever get nervous about this, right now, being the pinnacle of my career? Yeah, I do. At the end of filming every movie I think,

'Wow, this could be the last one! Nice working with you!'"

Every men's magazine tells you how sexy she is, every women's magazine how stylish and independent-minded she is. Film reviews constantly acclaim her on-screen presence, her toughness and beguiling charm, her charisma; her distinctive voice and cooler-than-cool delivery. Off-screen she seems to flit between self-effacing, just-a-regular-gal candour and spinning playful, elaborate fantasy yarns just to keep us guessing. People want to know her favourite chocolate bar (Snickers) and favourite comedy (*Waiting For Guffman*). Her favourite decade for style? The Forties. In the Noughties the roles keep coming, bigger and bigger, for the five-foot-four Amazon: a BAFTA win, four Golden Globe nominations.

With her credibility established, and box-office potential seemingly capable of surviving speed bumps, advertisers snap her up for huge sums. Her romances fuel acres of celebrity gossip. She is without doubt one of the twenty-first century's first and most intriguing cinematic phenomena: a hip icon to a new generation, yet possessed of the timeless allure that distinguishes the star from the player.

Everybody loves her.

This is due in part to a great and effective publicity machine. It's also due in part to her languidly electric performances in some outstanding movies. And it has easily outlived the weaker films: already, she's in an excellent position in the immortality queue. She has succeeded in making the transition from just another promising starlet. She seems incapable of irritating us. She seems to have that quality – that extra thing. And while often she acts her age, she also undeniably has wisdom beyond her years.

LEFT **Hollywood's new wave: Leaving Venice in casual-chic mode.**

ABOVE **Bringing sexy back: Scarlett at the Independent Spirit Awards in Santa Monica, March 2003.**

"It's a great thing to get older and learn," she says. "I don't feel bound in any way by how many years I've lived. I identify just as much with my 86-year-old grandmother as I do with my sister.

"Being a person in the public eye is a performance in itself. It's important for people to buy into that idea."

Why have we bought into Scarlett Johansson, as opposed to, say, Gretchen Moll or Mandy Moore or Kate Bosworth or Claire Danes? And what have we bought into? Does she embody a spirit of contemporary young womanhood like no other, or has she just been lucky, well-advised and smart, and thus landed great roles? Is she a dash of Deneuve crossed with a pinch of Hayworth? Or is she, in fact, as one disenchanted critic pointed out, "box-office poison"? Has she truly capitalized on her early career zenith of 2003? Scarlett, managed by her mother, could soon replace the likes of Nicole Kidman, Julia

TOP LEFT **At the *In Good Company* world premiere in Hollywood, 2004.
The film showed a new side of the actress.**

BELOW LEFT **Planning the next move with mother/manager Melanie in
New York, 2004. The pair have always stayed very close.**

ABOVE **In Cannes for Woody Allen's *Match Point*, May 2005. Signing up
with Allen gave her a new kind of credibility.**

Roberts and (awkwardly enough) Cameron Diaz as Hollywood
heroine number one. Or she could use her self-possession, her
sang-froid bordering on smugness, to acquire art-house cult
status beyond compare. How did she get so strong, so powerful,
so quickly? Where is she from? Where is she going? What is it
about those movies? Who does she become in them, and how?
Is she in control?

Who is she?

1 *Scarlett Fever*

Born in 1984 in New York, New York, young Scarlett Marie has already achieved a cinematic career of stellar proportions, swiftly becoming an icon to both genders. Much utilized as the selling-face of glamorous products (Calvin Klein, L'Oréal and, er, Reebok) and described as "the new Marilyn Monroe" by *Vogue*, she has also proven her mettle as a quality thespian, starring in movies as diverse as the literary and intelligent (*Ghost World* [2001], Woody Allen features) and the noisy, gung-ho Michael Bay's *The Island* (2005). And of course alternative hip fare like the film that made her name known the world over, Sofia Coppola's much-lauded *Lost in Translation* (2003).

When Scarlett won the *Hollywood Reporter* YoungStar [sic] Award for her breakthrough role – complete with leg amputation – in 1998's *The Horse Whisperer*, directed by Robert Redford, she was just 14 years old. And it was her seventh movie. Almost as soon as she reached adulthood, her profile, as if it had been waiting politely but confidently for the right moment, boomed in prominence. Coolly understated turns in *Ghost World* and *The Man Who Wasn't There* (2001) started a rumble which exploded into a fully blown buzz when her 2003 role as Charlotte in *Lost in Translation*, opposite Bill Murray, made her a cover girl, a chic role model and arguably the face of a generation.

Following this breakthrough strongly with films like *Girl with a Pearl Earring* (2003), *Match Point* (2005), *The Black Dahlia*

LEFT **Stepping up in *The Horse Whisperer*, the 1998 film that convinced Hollywood of her potential, with Robert Redford.**

BELOW **Coolly iconic in *Lost In Translation*, Scarlett played an isolated American abroad struggling to adapt to Tokyo.**

ABOVE **With Benicio Del Toro. Despite scurrilous tabloid gossip, Johansson insists absolutely nothing untoward took place.**

(2006) and *The Prestige* (2006), she has rocketed ahead of her peers and made the movie world her oyster. It seems plum roles will be hers for the asking for the foreseeable future.

"I don't think there's any kind of preparation for sudden celebrity," she has said. "I think you almost have this slight nervous breakdown when that kind of media attention happens. I mean, you're doing the same kind of thing that you do all the time, only you have to make these weird adjustments. Like, you're buying a slice of pizza and somebody's outside photographing you. Which is weird; that's not normal! It's very uncomfortable."

She claims her worst vice is … cheese. She relaxes by lighting candles "all over the place".

Yet Scarlett has adapted with relative grace. Until recently she enjoyed a relationship with actor and *The Black Dahlia* co-star Josh Hartnett, although she's latterly been linked with Justin Timberlake. This after we thought she'd got the folly of providing gossip-column fodder out of her system, first with a minor rock star, then a minor film star (Jared Leto), then during a reported (but hotly denied) romp with Oscar-winner Benicio Del Toro, 17 years her senior (sex in an elevator, went the water-cooler rumour; she blames this story on a jealous newsman with a thwarted crush). Having announced that she couldn't imagine dating anyone under 30 ("I feel a connection to older men") and thereby launching a million dubious fantasies among males of a certain age, she then gushed about new-found happiness with Hartnett. Until Timberlake slithered along, cruelly passing the torch from the Diaz generation to the Johansson one …

"The most precious moment in life is when you're about to fall in love," Scarlett cooed, Hartnett-era. "You're lying in bed together and he's gazing at you and you're gazing at him and there's a sense that something truly wondrous is about to happen. It's a nervous moment – but it's exhilarating." This from a girl who admits to having had such a crush on David Hasselhoff as a kid that, when she collaborated with him on voice work for *The Spongebob Squarepants Movie* (2004), she "went all girly". Her other big teen crush? Patrick Swayze. Such taste!

She isn't always so syrupy. "I am very independent," she declares. "I can look after myself, though I still like a lot of love and care. I try not to talk about my personal relationships; it always ends up kicking you in the face. But I've read a lot of things about myself and thought, 'Wow! That girl sounds really saucy!' I see other actresses are proud of the way they look and show it off, but that's never

really been my style." Scarlett was famously so startled when she caught sight of a massive LA billboard of herself that she "screamed and slammed on the brakes". "I couldn't believe it," she adds.

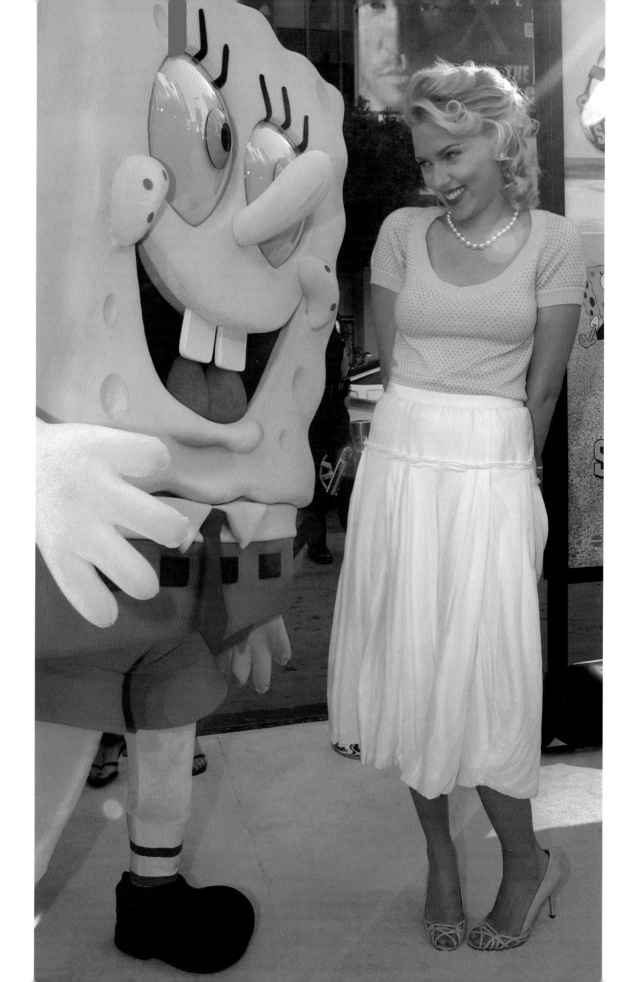

"It's very strange to see your cleavage the size of a brontosaurus. My breasts were *huge*. I had long hair, but, my goodness, I couldn't get past the cleavage!" Her acting, of course, has ensured that others have been able to make that leap – eventually.

The granddaughter of writer Ejner Johansson, Scarlett is of Polish/Danish descent. She has a twin brother, Hunter, three minutes her junior; an older brother, Adrian; and an older sister, Vanessa. She also has an older half-brother, Christian. Are you keeping up? Her father, Karsten Johansson, an architect/builder, was born in Denmark, while her mother, Melanie, comes from a Bronx-bred family of Polish roots. Her parents separated when Scarlett was 13, and she now visits Dad in New York (her own base) and Mom – now her manager and co-producer of several of her more recent films – in LA.

"I had a rich childhood," she says. "A lot of kids growing up have their creativity squashed and not accepted. But I was very lucky: my parents let me do my own thing."

Scarlett planned to attend Purchase College State University of New York to study film, and even as late as 2003 was applying to New York University, but the movie career dug in its heels. Since appearing in a *Late Night With Conan O'Brien* sketch on TV in 1993, aged just eight, she's paid her dues. She made her theatre debut off Broadway. There were the essential learning-curve movies before *The Horse Whisperer* got her galloping.

That voice helped. Her diction, onscreen, is so unorthodox, so shouldn't-work-but-does. She realizes others find her husky tones unusual, and one of her pet hates is being asked if she has a sore throat. But call that voice "distinctive" and she'll love you to bits.

As her onscreen personae demonstrate, Scarlett can portray both light and shade, eye-catching beauty and self-effacing ordinariness. She can play "period" or embody the essence of post-slacker modernity. She may have spent her twentieth birthday at Disneyland, but exhibited a less frothy side when she campaigned for Democrat candidate John Kerry against George W. Bush in the 2004 US presidential election. She makes telling contributions to children's

LEFT **Scarlett collaborated with David Hasselhoff on voice work for *The Spongebob Squarepants Movie* (2004).**

BELOW **With twin brother Hunter; they've joked they're about as identical as Arnold Schwarzenegger and Danny De Vito.**

ABOVE **With her mother and sister at the Golden Globes.**
The Johansson family is complex but fully functional.

RIGHT **Scarlett makes a political statement at the LA premiere**
of The Perfect Score, January 2004.

charities while remaining a staple on "hot lists" and "world's sexiest woman" polls. Not that she doesn't see the funny, even absurd, side of that. "Everyone in Hollywood is so damn skinny and you constantly feel like you're not skinny enough. But I have 'fat days', and although it's hard not to feel pressure in this industry, I accept that I'm never going to be rail thin."

After winning a BAFTA for *Lost in Translation*, she remarked frankly to *Vogue* that, "It felt normal. I've been working in this industry for as long as I can remember, so it felt like the award was, you know, 11 years in the making." For her, such brash matter-of-factness applies also to the art of acting itself. She claims she doesn't over-prepare, relying on spontaneity and the power of the script itself as much as possible.

She's a relaxed, savvy actor. "It feels right," she says, "but it's hard to explain how it happens".

Mercifully, on-screen magic is never easy to explain. Johansson has, in film, a fresh, arresting blend of perennial movie-star qualities – the twenty-first century Marilyn tags are fun, but they're hardly accurate – and dry, indie-ethic realism; in the brilliant *Ghost World*, for example, she seems almost too apathetic to mumble her lines. Her key films are notable for their contrasting range, from mainstream monsters to small-scale character studies. In *Lost in Translation*, what people reacted to was a presence more than a protagonist (not to mention her stumbling karaoke version of The Pretenders' "Brass in Pocket"). Young enough to remain mercurial and unpredictable, this is a girl who turned up to a *Vogue* shoot wearing, in the interviewer's words, "dirty jeans, black ballet pumps, trashy white porn-star sunglasses and a crocheted headscarf over her yellow blonde hair", then quipped, "Cut it all off. I'm trying to grow out a Ziggy Stardust mullet. Look: weird hair!"

She loves "everything about" making movies. Ten days after wrapping *Lost in Translation* in Tokyo and emotionally drained, she was on set in Holland for *Girl with a Pearl Earring*, in costume, with mop and broom, getting on with it. She knew then she'd come a long way fast since *Home*

Alone 3 (1997) and *My Brother the Pig* (1999). She won't be backsliding any time soon.

"You put a little piece of yourself into everything you do," she explains. "Even if you're playing some psychotic, some part of you is in that character – and hopefully, it's believable. I always come back to the fact that my own initial instincts are better than something I could construct in my mind."

Among Scarlett's forthcoming "instincts": an album of Tom Waits songs. Which will no doubt make Waits sound falsetto by comparison. And films galore, from *The Other Boleyn Girl* (in post-production at the time of writing) to *The Nanny Diaries* (2007). But did she really lose the *Mission: Impossible III* part after a disastrous meeting with Tom Cruise and a group of Scientologists?

"Tons of stuff comes to me, but a lot of it's awful. All those teenage slaying movies, and movies about girls who have deformities that become cheerleaders and then marry the prom king! Not for me ..."

We'll examine her key roles and films in this book. How did they achieve so much for her? How did she achieve so much via them? Which films worked, which were missteps? Which did she do for love, and which for profile? Who does she like working with, and why? She is an actor: what's her motivation?

At 22 years old, Scarlett Johansson is possibly the biggest "overnight success" story in movies this century. And it only took her 11 years of work to get there.

2 Scarlett as in O'Hara

The Professional Children's School in Manhattan, New York City, was founded in 1914. The following movie stars and television personalities are among its alumni: Sandra Dee, Mischa Barton, Ricki Lake, Christian Slater, Julia Stiles, Carrie Fisher, Sarah Michelle Gellar, Elliot Gould, Christopher Walken, Sarah Jessica Parker, Macaulay Culkin, Irene Cara, Christina Ricci, Tuesday Weld and Uma Thurman. Not to mention musicians such as Buddy Rich, Marvin Hamlisch and Anastasia. You could say it has a pretty good track record.

This is the "out-of-nowhere" whence the young actress Scarlett Johansson sprang. She was, as she has readily conceded, not disadvantaged. Her family was highly supportive of her creative urges. Scarlett is a twin. We could read something deep into that, possibly, but she doesn't. Her parents were of an artistic inclination. Drama, of a relaxed kind, runs in the family. Her sister Vanessa is also an actress. When Scarlett enrolled at this school, she'd already appeared in a couple of big movies.

Born on 22 November 1984, in New York City, Scarlett was from day one referred to as "cute" or "good-looking". Danish-born dad Karsten was a building contractor in Manhattan; mother Melanie looked after the family: Adrian, Vanessa and twins Scarlett and Hunter. Scarlett was born three minutes before Hunter. "They were the most important three minutes of my life," she has said, enigmatically. Today Hunter is six-foot-three with dark hair. Scarlett laughs that they're as much like twins as Arnold Schwarzenegger and Danny De Vito in that not altogether classic movie *Twins*. She also has a half-brother, Christian, who lives in Denmark with his mother.

This is where it becomes clear Scarlett was destined for great celluloid things. The family had a passion for tempestuous 1939 epic *Gone with the Wind*. Melanie Johansson decided that she herself must have been named

LEFT **Treading the boards in New York in the "24 Hour Plays", September 2001. Scarlett was "doing theatre" at a young age.**

RIGHT **A young Scarlett at the Independent Spirit Awards, 1997. Child stardom was no problem for the confident child.**

LEFT **Pushy mom syndrome? Surely not ... Scarlett with Melanie at a 1998 Fresh Air Fund benefit.**

ABOVE **Honing that "to-camera" gaze with her brother at a premiere for Danny Boyle's film *The Beach* in 2000.**

after the character Melanie Hamilton in the Selznick/Fleming classic; thus, Scarlett had to be named after Scarlett O'Hara, the temperamental anti-heroine of the Civil War love story (to whom Melanie Hamilton was friend/benefactor), as played uniquely by Vivien Leigh. Clark Gable may not, frankly, have given a damn, but O'Hara's emotional whirlwind certainly made an indelible impact on more than one generation of filmgoing females.

When asked about her religious affiliations, Johansson has said: "That's a very personal question. I would rather not answer." She has, however, at other times specified that she celebrates a "little of both" Christmas and Hanukkah, Christian and Jewish, although her parents are atheists.

She dislikes it when celebrities thank God in their award acceptance speeches.

It was a friend of mother Melanie's who inadvertently provided the push that started Scarlett on an acting career. So repeatedly did she comment on the children's blossoming beauty and suggest they go in for work in commercials that Melanie – like any proud, ambitious parent – couldn't resist the bait. She marched them all to an audition at an agency. It wasn't Scarlett the agents liked, originally, however: it was older brother Adrian. Melanie was pleased – until she saw the reactions of her other kids. Before they'd left the agent's office, young Scarlett, aged seven, went into hysterical fits. She didn't resent Adrian's luck, but seemed to know, even at this young age, that she desperately wanted to make it into movies (she has since said she knew she wanted to act from the age of three). Melanie previously

had no idea: this was a revelation. Millions of kids kick up a fuss and throw a tantrum when they don't instantly get what they crave, but this little girl really meant it!

With hindsight, Melanie admits that she did have an inkling.

Scarlett already loved watching movies ("Mom had a huge video collection, everything from *Oklahoma!* to *Chinatown*"), and among her favourite stars were glamour-pusses with a taste for exuberant comedy or showboating like Lucille Ball, Judy Garland and Rosalind Russell.

Melanie indulged young Scarlett in ballet lessons, thinking this would appease her yen for colourful dresses and the occasional bout of melodrama. But the movie-love grew ever stronger, perhaps fostered by the fact that these relatively liberal parents allowed the children to watch pretty much whatever they wanted from an early age. Scarlett has since conceded (or possibly bragged) that she saw *The Silence of the Lambs* (1991), the famous chiller starring Anthony Hopkins as Hannibal "the cannibal" Lecter, when she was just eight. Apparently Scarlett showed an interest that was strangely mature: she was already considering how such movies were made – the scale, the collaboration involved, the nuts and bolts. She was lapping up the glamour but also, crucially, wondering how the illusions were built and carried off. It became her obsession.

She soon ditched the ballet lessons and undertook the notoriously gruelling, competitive rounds of auditioning for parts – small parts, any parts – in TV, on stage, in advertisements, anything. Once she sat waiting for hours before being told that what the producers really wanted was a small Chinese boy. She has since recalled that she was prone to trying too hard, sometimes putting prospective employers off by her over-eagerness. And she didn't take rejection well. There was one incendiary tantrum on the New York subway, after which Melanie decided they would hunt solely for film work from that day forth. And succumbing to Scarlett's constant demands, she enrolled her at the well-

respected Lee Strasberg Theatre Institute for Young People, where her daughter studied from ages 8–11.

Scarlett was the youngest in her class, yet undertook studies of Stanislavsky's method – no mean task for one so fresh-faced. She gained priceless experience, acting in front of classmates and audiences. After just half one semester, she was promoted to the "young adult" sessions. Maturity and determination (not to mention talent) beyond her years were boosting her rockets. That throaty voice helped rather than hindered; she fitted in just fine.

In 1993 she appeared in a sketch on TV show *Late Night with Conan O'Brien*. Soon she was performing in a play off-Broadway, at Playwrights Horizons, in a small speaking role. The play was *Sophistry*, written by Jonathan Marc Sherman, and her leading man was Ethan Hawke (Hawke later went on to fame in movies such as *Training Day* [2001] and *Alive* [2003], and was to marry Uma Thurman).

Aged just ten, Scarlett landed her first movie role in *North* (1994), by director Rob Reiner. The film was, through no fault of hers, a critical and commercial disaster – no one can ever say she hasn't paid her dues, especially as some critics labelled it "the worst film ever made" – not the last time Scarlett would feature in a movie granted such a title.

Reiner had a terrific track record up to this point. In the years leading up to *North* going south, he'd directed such much-loved and diverse gems as *This is Spinal Tap* (1984), *Stand by Me* (1986), *When Harry Met Sally* (1989), *Misery* (1990) and *A Few Good Men* (1992). His directing career never truly recovered from this confused and confusing flop, however. Based on a script by comic writer Alan Zweibel, it attempted to tell the fable of a young boy, North (Elijah Wood, later star of *The Lord of The Rings* trilogy), who feels neglected by his rich, preoccupied parents (*Seinfeld* stars Jason Alexander and Julia Louis-Dreyfuss). He takes out a lawsuit against them, and a loopy judge (Alan Arkin) grants him the freedom to find "parents" he prefers, within two months. If he fails, he must return. Thus North embarks via Alaska, France and Texas on a "worldwide adventure".

It isn't much of an adventure. Narrated by Bruce Willis, who pops up in various guises alongside North, including those of a cowboy, a beach bum, a Fed Ex driver and

– weirdest of all – a pink Easter Bunny, the film meanders randomly. North auditions various would-be parents, and we meet a procession of indulgent and often preposterous star cameos. Among those briefly showing up to impress Reiner are such well-known names as Jon Lovitz, Dan Aykroyd, . Kathy Bates (as an Eskimo), and Kelly McGillis (as an Amish woman, thus parodying her performance in the Harrison Ford romance Witness [1985]). Scarlett eventually shows up as Laura Nelson (her dad's played by the late John Ritter, her mother by Faith Ford), of Bedford, a sun-baked suburb. North takes to the Nelsons; it's debatable whether we do. Scarlett doesn't have much of a part, although obviously it was key to her career in terms of getting her on the map.

Elijah Wood was the youngster nominated for awards here, but much funnier is the fact that North was nominated, embarrassingly, for no fewer than six "Razzies": the Razzies being the industry's joke ceremony celebrating the year's worst movies. Film, director, screenplay, Willis, Aykroyd and Bates all won a name-check here. North was swiftly buried

before it could bury any more careers. And thus, ironically, Scarlett Johansson's own film career was launched. Thankfully, this was just the start of young Scarlett's long haul. From North, the only way was up. Soon, to the dismay of her New York school, which was growing frustrated at her necessary absences, she had another movie part, alongside no less durable a screen icon than Sean Connery. Just Cause (1995), written by Jeb Stuart and based on a John Katzenbach novel, was originally supposed to have been directed by Canadian Norman Jewison (best known for The Cincinnati Kid [1965] and The Thomas Crown Affair [1968]), but when he pulled out, Connery persuaded his good friend Arne Glimcher to take over the project.

Just Cause was a murder-mystery thriller with bundles of far-fetched twists: arguably too many for its own good. In a swampy, muggy Florida town, Bobby Earl (Blair Underwood)

BELOW **The cast of** *North*, **with Scarlett bottom right and a young** ***The Lord Of The Rings*** **star, Elijah Wood (centre).**

is on Death Row, facing the electric chair for the murder of a young girl which took place eight years ago. He calls in Connery's Paul Armstrong, a Harvard law professor vehemently opposed to capital punishment in principle, to help prove his innocence. Armstrong's not sure whether to take up the cause, but his wife (played by one-time Mrs Spielberg, Kate Capshaw) eggs him on. When Armstrong does uncover a few secrets, the local police, headed by Laurence Fishburne as the sheriff, don't want to know. They think they already have the guilty party. And maybe they have. We're kept guessing by the great Ed Harris's over-the-top turn as a convicted psychopathic killer, as well as the convoluted plot.

As leading US critic Roger Ebert put it: "*Just Cause* starts out strong and then, boy, does it jump the rails …"

The final pay-offs are as annoying as they are revelatory. Scarlett plays the daughter of Connery and Capshaw, and endures some creepy moments when the real villain terrorizes her. She has said that working with Connery – for many movie fans, the greatest of all James Bonds – was a fantastic experience for such a novice, and that Fishburne, too, was generous with helpful advice and encouragement. Scarlett recalls when she and Fishburne were sitting together on a plane once, and he told her she had to decide if she wanted to be an actress or a movie star. She'd have to make the choice sooner rather than later. Scarlett says she's kept these words of wisdom in mind regarding her career ever since.

Drew Barrymore also later helped her along the road with the benefit of lessons learned from her career trajectory from child star to off-the-rails wild child to comeback industry player.

"Whatever you do," Barrymore said, "don't go into acting for the fame, because you're gonna end up unhappy."

Scarlett has been quoted as saying, "And I don't really think you can 'become' an actress – you *are* an actress." Her next few films were to be (relatively) less high profile, which probably gave her a chance to keep a sense of balance, collect her breath, and continue to learn her craft. Her whirlwind entrance to the movie-making arena was placed, sensibly, on pause.

School had been frowning on Scarlett's extra-curricular work rate, so around this time, with her mother's support (it's said that from her mother, now a showbiz mover and shaker, she has picked up a fast-talking, sarcastic "Jewish sensibility") she transferred to a private establishment: the Professional Children's School mentioned earlier. It was an ideal fit. She was to visit this superstar training academy – with, obviously, breaks for filming – until graduating in early 2002, often having additional tuition on the set of her movies.

What constitutes a breather in Scarlett's career, however, still cuts a break-neck pace by most standards. The roles kept coming, thick and fast. The film world had seen what she could do, and was already hugely impressed.

The spark was lit. The flames would come.

LEFT **Early pal of Johansson, Drew Barrymore similarly grew up on screen, surviving a rocky patch to consolidate her status.**

3 *Independent Spirit*

*O*f Scarlett's next three films, two were romantic comedies by writer/director Eric Schaeffer, but the other was vital in propelling her to global fame, as it won her an Independent Spirit Award nomination and, more significantly, was greatly admired by a young viewer and cinephile who aspired to following in her father's directional footsteps. The fan's name was Sofia; her father was Francis Ford Coppola, the legend behind *The Godfather* (1972) and *Apocalypse Now* (1979).

LEFT **Twelve-year-old Scarlett in Craig Schaeffer's *If Lucy Fell*, 1996 – another stepping stone for the fast-learning girl.**

BELOW **Accepting the plaudits with *Lost In Translation* director Sofia Coppola at the Film Critics Association Awards, LA, January 2004.**

Less than apocalyptic was *If Lucy Fell* (1996), a harmless, fluffy rom-com that marked Scarlett's next onscreen appearance. It did boast a mostly soon-to-be-big-name cast, again proving the young actress's knack for networking by default. In this "comedy for the romantically challenged", Joe (Schaeffer) and Lucy (Sarah Jessica Parker, soon to star in *Sex and the City*) are former college friends, now room-mates, pushing 30. Lucy suggests that if the pair don't find romance within the month they should fulfil an old pact, originally made in jest, of jumping off the Brooklyn Bridge together. This deadline prompts bumbling Joe to act upon his crush on his neighbour (out-of-his-league supermodel Elle Macpherson), while Lucy undergoes dates with handsome Robert John Burke and loopy dreadlocked wannabe artist Ben Stiller (a typically over-the-top and often hilarious early turn from Stiller, as the infuriating yet endearing "Bwick"). Of course, we're led into hoping true love wins the day.

The problem is that Schaeffer isn't an easy guy to like, while "annoying" has always been S.J.P.'s middle name. "Would you drink my spit?" she asks. "No, I don't think I'd be interested in that," he replies. *We're* certainly not interested in that. Scarlett shows up as Emily, one of teacher Schaeffer's brightest young charges. And if you don't buy Schaeffer as a teacher, how about Parker as a therapist? We do buy Johansson as wise beyond her years. Naturally.

In *The New York Times*, Janet Maslin scoffed: "Elle Macpherson swoons over Schaeffer and calls him 'a cute, smart, sexy, good-looking guy' – perhaps labouring under the misconception that he is the new Woody Allen. True, he's made a bittersweet romantic comedy with a New York setting, but that's as far as the resemblance goes." Ironically, Scarlett was later to become the muse of the "old" Woody Allen.

"This is painfully cute," the review continued. "On many occasions you may wish they'd just go ahead and jump off that bridge."

A year later Scarlett shone very briefly as "little girl" (not her most well-known role) in *Fall*, another Schaeffer writer/ director/star ego trip. Less comedic and more of

ABOVE **Not very acclaimed thesps Amanda De Cadenet and Eric Schaeffer in** *Fall*, **which gave Scarlett another notch on her résumé.**

RIGHT **Lisa Krueger's film** *Manny And Lo* **(1996) saw Scarlett winning praise for a mature-beyond-her-years performance.**

a passionate, highly sexed romance, it studied the potential for love between a cab driver and a supermodel. "I see you everywhere," says "charismatic" Michael (Schaeffer) to "beautiful" European model Sarah (Amanda De Cadenet). "I see you nowhere," she retorts, but is attracted to his animal magnetism. British fans will recall De Cadenet as a slightly useless TV presenter and serial girlfriend of rock stars. They get jiggy while her husband Phillippe (Rudolf Martin) is abroad, but can she leave her glossy superficial world behind and commit to a penniless man? Schaeffer lays on the philosophical and literary references, but his cockiness repels, as does the fact that much of the film seems to be telling us how great he is in bed. "I just want to make you come," he heavy-breathes at the reliably gormless De

Cadenet. You can almost see him wondering if this movie will get him dates. It's one of those films you either love or hate.

It didn't do Johansson any harm, however. Between her two shimmies for Schaeffer, she'd taken on an entirely more challenging role – a role which constituted her next major step on the road to fame. *Manny and Lo* (1996) was written and directed by Lisa Krueger, who'd earned her spurs as an associate and script supervisor to Jim Jarmusch, the *auteur* behind *Down by Law* (1986) and *Mystery Train* (1989). Scarlett played the titular Manny, and narrated.

Aleksa Palladino was Laurel ("Lo"), 16-year-old sister to Amanda ("Manny")'s 11-year-old. The pair run away from their drunk, stoned mother and alternative adopted parents and, like a kind of adolescent Thelma and Louise, take to the

road. Lo hot-wires a car, steals supplies. They sleep in model homes or under any free roof they can find. Hassled once too often, they decide – upon learning that Lo is pregnant – to deal with the crisis by kidnapping Elaine (Mary Kay Place), a baby-supply-store worker. Elaine, lonely, becomes fond of them. There's a growing ersatz mother-daughters situation. In a country cabin, a touching, dysfunctional relationship develops among the trio in an unpredictable, whimsical tale involving believable, complex characters.

Scarlett again displays her older-than-her-years insouciance.

"Number-one rule," she mumbles as narrator: "keep moving, and you won't get nailed."

When Manny asks Elaine why she has no family, the reply she returns is: "I'm afraid I was not terribly … unified … as a younger person." Later Elaine remarks to Manny, the "sensible" foil to her maverick sibling, "While I cannot condone this kidnapping, I do think you're a very fine young lady."

"Really?" says Manny, as Johansson shows cute comic timing. "Thanks!"

Produced by the team behind David O. Russell's indie hits *Spanking the Monkey* (1994) and *Flirting with Disaster* (1996), *Manny and Lo* drew great reviews.

Sofia Coppola was bowled over by it: "I always liked her in *Manny and Lo*, as a cute little girl with that husky voice."

Its atmospheric score by John Lurie was a plus. Scarlett got her Independent Spirit nomination for Best Female Lead. Krueger and Place were also nominated, while Krueger won an Open Palm Award. In the *LA Times*, Kenneth Turan called it, "A perfectly pitched oddball comedy that reveals a wholly original sensibility," while *The New York Times* hailed it as, "A warm, fabulously unsentimental comedy. One of the finds of the year."

In terms of Scarlettology studies, there's something else fascinating about *Manny and Lo*. The family the two sisters watch on a golf course in one scene are played by Scarlett's

BELOW *Home Alone 3* (1997) may not have been the greatest work of Scarlett's young career.

RIGHT **Scarlett's surprise fourteenth birthday party – even her acting chops can't hide the confusion.**

real-life parents, brother and sister. After this film, Melanie Johansson, who'd always had faith, must have known her daughter was going places.

The first place she was to go, however, was home. That is, to star in *Home Alone 3*, the 1997 sequel to the Macaulay Culkin box-office smashes. Written, like its predecessors, by John Hughes (still best known as the man behind 1980s teen classics *The Breakfast Club* [1985] and *Pretty in Pink* [1986]), and directed by Raja Gosnell (who went on to the equally broad and cartoonish *Big Momma's House* [2000] and *Scooby Doo* [2002]), this boy-in-peril-fights-intruders comedy starred a new hero: eight-year-old Alex Pruitt, as played by Alex D. Linz, replacing Culkin. (It never made him as big a celebrity as Culkin, though; perhaps a role which lumbered him with chickenpox wasn't the best Hollywood calling card.) Scarlett, now 13, played his big sister, Molly. If *Manny and Lo* was a marvellous showcase for her acting talents, this, well, wasn't. As a kid, it was her first kids' movie, after several roles in "grown-up" movies. Spies plant microchips in a toy car; the toy car winds up in Alex's house while his parents are away … you can guess the rest. Alex saves the day, with mock violence, slapstick aplenty and lots of loud crash-bang-wallop. Nevertheless, critics agreed that, as kids' entertainment, it was fine, and less of a let-down, after the freshness of the franchise's original, than *Home Alone 2*. And Scarlett was thus far surviving adolescence (and avoiding typecasting) better than fellow Professional Children's School student Macaulay Culkin had done.

When equally promising young actress Natalie Portman bravely or foolishly dropped out of her next movie role (there were scheduling delays and difficulties) to act on Broadway in *The Diary Of Anne Frank*, another window of opportunity opened for Johansson. It was a big movie and a big part: Robert Redford's *The Horse Whisperer*. This was her seventh movie, but her on-screen credit read: "Introducing Scarlett Johansson".

RIGHT **The buzz around Johansson could now clearly be heard: from Robert Redford's *The Horse Whisperer*.**

4 "Introducing

Scarlett Johansson ..."

*H*aving auditioned for the lead in the remake of family chestnut *The Parent Trap* (1998) and seen the old Hayley Mills role go to wild-child-in-waiting Lindsay Lohan, Scarlett was discussing the best strategies for a work-education balance when a whisper became a roar. She'd landed the part of Grace in 1998's *The Horse Whisperer*, one of the most anticipated movies of its year.

Nicholas Evans's novel had been an American best-seller and critics' favourite. The inevitable film version was much talked about, with rumours that Clint Eastwood might try to make it in a similar manner to *The Bridges Of Madison County* (1995; also based on a briefly ubiquitous book), or even that Steven Spielberg may be getting involved. (Barely

a major book-to-film adaptation goes by without Spielberg's name being linked at some stage). When former heartthrob actor-turned-Sundance Institute/Festival guru Robert Redford signed on to star and direct, the reaction was positive: Redford was seen as a safe pair of hands and had a fine track record. In 1980 he'd won the Best Director Oscar for *Ordinary People*, and *A River Runs Through It* (1992) and *Quiz Show* (1994) kept his stock high. The casting of Kristin Scott Thomas as his love interest was a coup; the haughty beauty had herself recently been Oscar-nominated for her work in Anthony Minghella's stirring *The English Patient* (1996).

Also in the cast were such steady performers as Sam Neill, Dianne Wiest (a Woody Allen favourite) and Chris

LEFT **An adolescent Scarlett, still growing into the face we all now know so well.**

BELOW **With Robert Redford and Kristin Scott Thomas, star of Anthony Minghella's *The English Patient*, in *The Horse Whisperer*.**

Cooper. Shoring up an already impressive team were director of photography Robert Richardson (regular ally of Oliver Stone and Martin Scorsese, and later Quentin Tarantino) and screenwriters Eric Roth (hot on the back of *Forrest Gump* [1984]) and Richard Lagravenese. This surely had "Oscar fodder" written all over it. That it then somehow sank under its own *gravitas* had nothing to do with Johansson, who shone like the golden glow Redford shot himself in for almost three hours.

The story's basic theme is: country and nature equals good, city and pressure equals bad. Out riding in snowy woods, a girl (Scarlett as Grace McLean) and her horse Pilgrim are hit by a truck in a terrible accident.

The horse is crippled and left a nervous wreck; Grace has to have her foot and part of her leg amputated. "No one will ever want me now," muses Grace.

Her Manhattanite mother Annie (Scott Thomas) is a workaholic magazine editor (apparently modelled on *The New Yorker's* boss Tina Brown). She refuses to have the horse put down, reading of a famed "horse whisperer" in Montana who mysteriously heals troubled animals. When the whisperer, Tom Booker (Redford), isn't interested over the phone, Annie impetuously drives both daughter and horse to Big Sky country to see him. She feels, somewhat irrationally, that if the horse gets better, so will Grace.

Once the two women impose themselves upon Booker's cattle ranch, bonding and healing does indeed begin, albeit slowly (this is a long, long film). Booker cures the horse by staring at it a lot. This seems to work with both females, too, as the camera seems convinced that Redford is still the golden boy of his 1960s and '70s roles. Annie lets her hyperactivity dissolve into the mountain air, falling in love with the cowboy; Grace becomes less frustrated and more positive.

LEFT **Scarlett in a reflective mood on the Manhattan set of** *The Horse Whisperer*.

RIGHT **Perfecting that celebrated steely glare – a little work to be done yet, perhaps.**

While, for many reviewers, the relationship between chilly Scott Thomas and mellow Redford never convincingly gels, the rapport between his Booker and Johansson's Grace feels more authentic and human. Grace is sullen at first and won't engage (Scarlett gives good "sullen"), but Tom grants her respect and patience. When she says she can't drive the ranch pick-up truck, he chuckles, "No time like the present to start." She's encouraged by his calmness and faith. Tom and Annie's love may or may not be fated to endure, but Grace's recovery will.

Tom: "It's like the boy I knew just went away somewhere ..."
Grace: "I know where he goes."
Tom: "I know you do. But don't you disappear."

Scarlett wasn't about to disappear. The film, however, disappointed: its indulgences were too downbeat for most. Maybe young audiences didn't want romance between "older" people any more. The only Oscar nomination it was to receive was for Best Song, and this after a score commissioned from the great John Barry had been rejected. For all its sumptuous scenery, the film also included one glaring continuity error: when Grace wakes up in hospital after the accident, there's a bandage on her forehead. Seconds later, there isn't.

Scarlett was blameless for the epic's failings, and Redford reiterated what many industry insiders already lauded her for when he opined that "She's 13 going on 30." She confirmed this smartness when, in an interview, she recalled the director attempting to get her to summon up dread and fear as the truck that was to injure her approached. "It's coming closer, closer," he urged sincerely. Scarlett smirked that what had run through her mind was, *This isn't scary. What this is is every middle-aged woman's dream come true.*

Her work was recognized across Hollywood, and her YoungStar [sic] Award ensued. Strangely, further work offers – or at least of the standard the ambitious actress now desired – did not instantly flood in. She moaned of being offered plenty

RIGHT **Robert Redford receives sage-like advice from the talented youngster on the set of** *The Horse Whisperer*.

38

> ❝ *I think we were all a little intimidated by her. Most people have self-doubt at some point in their lives or work. Scarlett doesn't have that.* ❞
>
> Joel Coen

of "horseback champions with fatal diseases". Or those staples thrust at teenage stars: "sexy girls menaced by psycho-killers in masks". Her mother, now manager, had the gumption not to panic. It helped that the Johanssons weren't broke. While she waited for that "right" role, Scarlett did take one to kill time, and it isn't one that will ever feature among her top on-screen achievements. Maybe she just needed to blow off steam after all that horse-healing earnestness. For it was now that this "young artist" threw herself into that slice of aesthetic genius known as *My Brother the Pig*.

We won't spend too much time regarding this 1999 masterpiece, but on the bright side it gave Scarlett a lead role, as a "pretty normal teenage girl, for a change". Directed by Erik Fleming, it was a children's comedy wherein 14-year-old Kathy Caldwell (Johansson) sees her obnoxious nuisance of a brother George (Nick Fuoco) magically turned into a – yes, you guessed it – pig. Be careful what you wish for! So she, along with friends and the voodoo-plying nanny responsible for this Kafka-esque metamorphosis (played by rising star Eva Mendes), has to travel to Mexico to get the spell reversed before her parents return from vacation. Only Nanny's grandmother can fix things. Judge Reinhold plays the dad, and Scarlett's *Home Alone 3* buddy Alex D. Linz is involved.

LEFT **Seemingly devoid of self-doubt, arriving at a Czech Republic film festival screening of *Ghost World*, July 2001.**

ABOVE **Growing up in public. The star-to-be in 1997, just before fame came to town.**

Although the pig has to keep an eye out for greedy butchers, this is no *Babe*. It's not even a *Babe 2: Pig in the City*.

As a showcase for young new stars, including Linz, the romp did its job.

"She's blossoming fast into one of the best of the younger set," noted one commentator.

In a matter of a few years, this young actor would be telling interviewers and camera crews that the red carpet might look fabulous, but "in reality, it's frantic and surreal".

Johansson soon found the meatier showcases she was seeking. Two excellent movies by any standards, with Scarlett at their heart, emerged next, in Terry Zwigoff's *Ghost World* and the Coen Brothers' *The Man Who Wasn't There*. As the twenty-first century dawned and Scarlett approached adulthood, she had very nearly already arrived.

5 *"The New Lauren Bacall"*

At 16, Scarlett Johannson found herself described for the first time (at least in reviews) as "a hottie". Her next two back-to-back roles were to establish the former child almost-star as a knowing teenager, faintly aware of her blossoming sexuality while subverting stereotypes. In *The Man Who Wasn't There* (2001) she became, not for the last time, a seductress. But it was in Zwigoff's exquisitely cool *Ghost World* (2001) that she first displayed the sceptical, self-assured nonchalance that to this day remains such a fundamental part of her unique, possibly generation-defining appeal.

Ghost World is a true one-off, its tag-line "Accentuate the negative". This funny, cynical cult movie merits all the accolades heaped upon it, and much of its bleak, wise-ass charm is down to the pairing of Johansson with Thora Birch to embody two prematurely jaded teenage friends, sympathetic misfits and wilful outsiders. Birch is the star, but Johansson's a sterling sidekick and foil.

It was based on the graphic novels of Daniel Clowes, one of the best artists in the genre. His other works – like *David Boring*, or *Art School Confidential* (more recently filmed by Zwigoff) – are similarly melancholy, poetic and satirical hymns to the disaffected. Zwigoff had made a documentary about another fabled cartoonist, Robert

LEFT **Coming in from the cold at a Jill Stuart Fall Fashion show, New York public library, February 2003.**

BELOW **Terry Zwigoff's *Ghost World* (2001), where she graduated in so many ways. Here with co-star Thora Birch.**

Crumb, in 1994, but although *Crumb* was highly praised, *Ghost World* was his debut feature. He soon establishes a mood in which individual scenes and snappy one-liners and putdowns can flourish.

Enid (Birch) and Rebecca (Johansson) are best pals with an attitude problem. Graduating from high school, the summer looming, they don't want to enter a world of materialism, malls and corporate blandness. They can't work out what to do instead, but yearn for a more bohemian, alternative way of life. Accurately, they despise the way the planet's turning into a consumerist theme park. They nurture a vague crush on Brad Renfro.

"I think I'm going crazy from sexual frustration," grumbles Enid.
"And you haven't heard of the miracle of masturbation?" mocks Rebecca.

We're a long way from *The Horse Whisperer* or *Home Alone 3* here. We're in a different world. So's Scarlett.

Enid attends summer art school under eccentric teacher Illeana Douglas, and loses her vacation job in a cinema. She's not the best salesperson. Asked if she serves alcohol, she replies: "I wish. Actually, you wish. After about five minutes of this movie, you'll wish you'd had ten beers." The girls meet 40-something loser Seymour (the impeccable Steve Buscemi) who obsessively collects old jazz and blues records in lieu of any human relationships. Enid, initially sarcastic, warms to him.

"He's the exact opposite of everything I really hate," she confides to Rebecca. "In a way, he's such a clueless dork, he's almost kinda cool."

"That guy is many things," responds Rebecca, using that nasal Johansson voice to the max, "but he's definitely not cool".

The quality of "cool" is much discussed by the two teens.

"This is so bad it's almost good," muses Rebecca.

Enid corrects her: "It's so bad it's gone past good and back to bad again."

As Enid becomes closer to Seymour, the two girls drift apart, and to Enid's dismay a slightly jealous Rebecca shows signs of giving up rebellion to embrace social convention. There's a reluctant part-acceptance that "adulthood" – and also heartbreak, a tidal feeling that even the most finely tuned ironic distance can't always overcome – may be inevitable.

Birch, perfectly pitched throughout, dominates the movie. Riding high on the global success of Sam Mendes's *American Beauty* (1999), this was a bold choice for her, and she gained 20 pounds for the role. Johansson, however, proved again that she had real presence onscreen. Free from the constraints of cute kiddiedom, she was able to display, casually, her innate "alternative" aura.

"Some people are OK," reckons Rebecca, "but mostly I just feel like poisoning everybody."

If Rebecca ultimately betrays Enid, it's not without much intelligent consideration and artful ambivalence.

Ghost World was a left-of-centre hit upon its 2001 release, and much garlanded. Scarlett won a Toronto Film Critics award and a Chlotrudis Award for Best Supporting Actor. She was also nominated for an Online Film Critics Society Prize, and people sat up and paid attention to that sandpaper voice; she saw, with some bemusement, comparisons to Lauren Bacall emerge. Reviews glowed: "One of the best movies of the year," reckoned *Time Out*. BBC man Jonathan Ross urged, "I don't recommend you see it – I *insist* you do." Even *The Guardian's* Peter Bradshaw, habitually harsh, was forced to note its "sadness, lugubriousness and comically humane sense of the ordinary" and its "tough, wised-up sassiness". *Rolling Stone* praised its "dark wit and nuance". It even gained an Oscar nomination for Best Adapted Screenplay. Zwigoff went on to make the incomparably wicked *Bad Santa* (2003) with one Billy Bob Thornton, who was to be Scarlett's next co-star.

In 2000, Ethan and Joel Coen were among the hottest movie-helming names in the world. Since the early 1980s their quirky, genre-crossing films had made them critically revered and commercially appealing. Movies such as *Raising Arizona* (1987), *Barton Fink* (1991) and *Fargo* (1996) had combined humour and enigma, while 1998's *The Big Lebowski* remains a huge cult favourite to this day. While making an earlier film, *The Hudsucker Proxy* (1984), the brothers had come up with a story, originally known between them as "The Barber Project", which they now elected to film. Billy Bob Thornton and Frances McDormand took the lead roles, with *The Sopranos* pivot James Gandolfini also cast. In the role of teenage temptress Birdy Abundas, they cast the fastest-rising young woman in Hollywood, Scarlett Johansson, now eager to confirm she could handle adult roles of depth and risk.

Set in 1949 in the small town of Santa Rosa, California (a real place), *The Man Who Wasn't There* set out to reinvent the *film noir* genre. This being the Coens, the reinvention was full of tangents, curveballs and innovation. It was filmed in colour, then printed in black and white via special processing. Its storyline was somehow both beautifully simple and ridiculously convoluted, incorporating adultery, blackmail, foul play, invented war heroics, shaved legs, Beethoven, Heisenberg, celibacy and lust. Oh, and UFOs and aliens.

BELOW **Teen temptress Birdy in the Coens' *The Man Who Wasn't There* (2001), where she caught the eye of Billy Bob Thornton.**

At its centre is narrator Ed Crane (Thornton, superb as ever), who cuts hair in his in-laws' barbershop. His neglectful wife (McDormand) is a borderline-alcoholic, and Ed suspects that she may be having an affair with her boss, Big Dave (Gandolfini). Big Dave has money to invest; Ed reckons he could use that money – a little blackmail may be in order. But murder intrudes, and soon Ed isn't as invisible as he thought he was.

It's a compelling, original film, for all its subtle, in-joke references to *Double Indemnity* (1944), *The Big Sleep* (1946) and *The Postman Always Rings Twice* (1946).

Thornton delivers his lines deftly. "Me, I don't talk much, I just cut the hair" and "My wife and I have not performed the sex act in many years" have become movie-buff catchphrases.

He was not always so deadpan, however. When, at an office party, Ed Crane first watches teenage neighbour Birdy (Johansson) playing Beethoven on a grand piano, Thornton faked an erection as a practical joke. To his disappointment, only one of the prop crew noticed – otherwise the film may have included an extra few, uncalled-for, inches.

Scarlett, dark-haired and in period garb, is very much a sexual entity in the film. *Variety's* review noted quietly: "Johansson, much grown since *The Horse Whisperer*, is very good." Notwithstanding that, when she's first seen playing Beethoven, her hands are (as musicians have pointed out) in completely the wrong place to be playing the notes we hear. Birdy is a low-key tease, very *noir*, very enigmatic, but Crane is sorely tempted by this *faux*-innocent Lolita-type, eventually succumbing to her seduction techniques when she (rather less than innocently) performs oral sex on him in his car. "Heavens to Betsy, Birdy!" exclaims the simultaneously startled and delighted Crane.

The Man Who Wasn't There, which won an Oscar nomination for Roger Deakins's cinematography, is a more resonant, philosophical film than these snippets might suggest. It's not every film in which the protagonist

wonders whether human hair has soul. *The Guardian's* reviewer likened Thornton's performance to Gary Cooper or Henry Fonda, and called the film the Coens' masterpiece. "What a stunning, mesmeric movie this is. I can only hope that on Oscar night the Academy are not so cauterized with dumbness and cliché that they cannot recognize its originality and playful brilliance. The best American film of the year." Sadly, as the pinnacle of a tremendous run of features, it was to be the Coens' last great film to date. After this, their form dipped yawningly for star-vehicle froth like

RIGHT **Johansson is mysterious and *noir* in *The Man Who Wasn't There*, one of the Coen Brothers' finest films to date.**

Intolerable Cruelty (2003) and *The Ladykillers* (2004). We have to hope sincerely that their muse returns, for, when they're on their game, there's nobody quite like them, and one can't help but feel that the mature Scarlett Johansson would make an ideal Coen leading lady. She has the ambivalence, the complexity, the air of the unknowable.

"I think we were all a little intimidated by her," Joel Coen has said, with awe. "Most people have self-doubt at some point in their lives or work. Scarlett doesn't have that." At one point the Coens suggested that her character eat sunflowers seeds during a scene. According to Thornton, she just gave them a withering gaze, and they left the room, mumbling apologies.

Scarlett's next film, *An American Rhapsody*, gave her a demanding role in a well-intended but faintly drippy film. Released in 2001, it had taken years to come to fruition. Its writer/director Eva Gardos had been a casting director on Francis Ford Coppola's *Apocalypse Now*. Gardos had also edited Peter Bogdanovich's *Mask* (1994) and Barbet Schroeder's *Barfly* (1987). Colleen Camp, acting in Coppola's

Vietnam War epic, had been enchanted by Gardos's true-life tales of growing up in the States as a Hungarian émigré, and encouraged her to make a film on the subject. Ultimately, Camp produced *An American Rhapsody* and took a small supporting role in it. For all its sentimentality ("One family's struggle for survival, for justice, for freedom"), it was moderately well-received, although *The Washington Post* called it "crude, a little forced and flat".

It begins in 1950s Budapest, where a young couple (Nastassja Kinski and Tony Goldwyn) are compelled to flee the oppressive Communist regime and hot-foot it to the USA, land of the free. They have to leave their baby daughter Suzanne with a foster couple. Years on, Suzanne is brought to America by the Red Cross and reunites with her parents in LA. The 15-year-old (now embodied by Scarlett) suffers from a mind-boggling culture clash, and is confused by customs, boys, clothes and family values.

"I am not a child!" she shrieks at Kinski. "You don't know who I am!" She smokes, she sulks, she shouts.

The troubled rebel demands that she's allowed to visit Hungary again to find her roots and fathom her true identity. "It's funny, but all those years I felt like I didn't belong anywhere …"

The inexperienced Gardos relies on heavy-handed Stalinist-era symbolism too often, but Scarlett does what she can with the role, her persona granting life to even the dullest platitudes. She and Kinski play decently together, although Johansson's already so self-confident that she tends to overpower Goldwyn (the father) and make him seem more weak and puny than the story intends. There are some classic bloopers – a huge satellite dish adorns a house in what's supposed to be 1950s LA, steam trains chug through 1960s Hungary – but Johansson's authority is such that she overcomes even the Hungarians-have-bad-haircuts-but-Americans-have-cool-ones corniness. She's one tough cookie. At the Young Artists Awards, the ensemble picked up a prize and Scarlett (this was becoming a habit, already)

LEFT **Johansson as Suzanne, torn between Hungarian roots and modern USA in Eva Gardos's *An American Rhapsody*, 2001.**

won Best Actress. There was one catch: she shared the title with Emma Watson, the even younger star of the latest *Harry Potter* flick, which may have niggled at the *gravitas* of the award somewhat. To her irritation, Scarlett didn't instantly become inundated with worthwhile offers. Hollywood pressed on with its bizarre custom of casting good-looking 20-somethings as teenagers.

Nevertheless Scarlett was finding her place in the world with greater ease and aplomb, and dealing with modern American craziness more guilefully than that poor Hungarian émigré. Then came a serious conundrum, one which probes the innermost psyche of the contemporary Western world: how do you deal with giant mutant man-eating spiders?

Eight-Legged Freaks (2002) may not go down in history as an envelope-pushing work of raw genius, but its campy horror schtick introduced Johansson to a new audience, an audience which screamed and laughed a lot, sometimes simultaneously.

"Do you hate spiders? Do you really hate spiders? Well they don't like you, either!"

An homage to 1950s B-movies, New Zealander Ellory Elkayem's feature (working title "Arac Attack") was developed from his own short, *Larger Than Life* (1996). He had the producers of *Godzilla* (1998) and *Independence Day* (1996) on his team, so the effects were nothing if not special.

The script was deliberately dumb. In a small rural Arizona mining town called Prosperity (yes, the clichés rain down thick and fast), a contaminated-chemicals spillage causes an army of spiders to grow to the size of cars overnight. The townsfolk have to take up arms against this sea of arachnids. There's dopey David Arquette, sheriff Sam (the always undervalued Kari Wuhrer), her rebellious teenage daughter Ashley (Scarlett), her boyfriend, and a paranoid radio-show host (Doug E. Doug). Can they beat off the icky intruders in "the biggest, nastiest mutant spider movie of all time"? (Well, apart from 1990's *Arachnophobia*, directed by Frank Marshall and starring Jeff Daniels and John Goodman, that is …)

"Originality ain't on the menu, but there's never a dull moment in this comic chiller," chuckled *Variety*. Many reviewers remarked on Scarlett's burgeoning sex appeal – at one point she's pinioned against a wall by a spider's web while minimally dressed – and awarded Wuhrer and Johansson "sexiest mother-daughter pairing" status. It was nominated for a Saturn Award as Best Horror Film, even though it was riddled with clangers: when a tent is supposedly moved by a spider-beast, you can see human hands pulling it along. The cast routinely get to holler such quality lines as "They're here! They're here!" and "So, you're telling me that a giant spider ate Gladys?"

Scarlett's best line comes during a heated row with Mom.

"Mom!" yells Ashley, archetypal grumpy teen-brat. "I'm not like you! I'm not gonna get pregnant at 16. I'm not gonna stay here for the rest of my life and be a trailer-trash sheriff!"

"Thanks for the flashback," deadpans Wuhrer, "I really didn't deserve that."

It's hard to deny that when *The Guardian* tutted that "Johansson, a potential A-lister, is ever so slightly slumming it here" it had something of a point. This raucous romp was never going to be the movie to send her supernova. That would be her next film.

LEFT *Eight-Legged Freaks* (2002) a work of cinematic genius, arguably – there are giant mutant spiders to be tussled with.

6 Lost in Translation

Two thousand and three was Scarlett's big year. Or rather, the first of her big years.

"This past year has been really insane, quite a whirlwind," she told Carlo Cavagna of AboutFilm, a movie website. "I've been really busy, pulled in a lot of directions, but it's great. I'm just trying to keep my head on straight."

Lost in Translation, directed by Sofia Coppola, was a winner from start to finish. You could lose yourself in it. While the initial media buzz may have focused on its signifiers of hip (East meets West very stylishly; that hottest of directors; that Kevin Shields/Brian Reitzell soundtrack), it proved to be a laconic, low-key *Brief Encounter* for an ad-fed generation. It's wryly funny, often moving, and very beautiful in a cool, uncloying manner. Coppola seems more confidently engaged with the material than she was on her dreamy, floaty, slightly overrated debut *The Virgin Suicides* (1999, which starred Josh Hartnett). Johansson worked wonders with a nebulous role (the whole film is nebulous and narcotic, in a terrific way). And Bill Murray? We'd always known he knew what he was doing, even though if you actually look at his filmography he's made two stinkers for every great movie. Here, he's perfect, expressing everything we knew he could express if he brought his A-game to the table. He's an unlikely romantic lead, which is the kind of romantic lead that gets you where it matters. And if it seems impossible to make an authentically romantic movie these days (when formulaic rom-coms have hacked down our disbelief from wherever we were suspending it), this is that movie.

Two strangers are stuck in Tokyo, a neurotic, neon paradise. Bob (Murray) is a jaded movie star, to his shame shooting a silly whisky commercial for big money. He can't connect, over disjointed phone calls and time zones, with his wife of 25 years. He watches TV in his hotel room, offends a call-girl, drinks. Improvises sketches with language barriers, running machines, swimming pools. He wonders where what's left of his life is going. The much younger Charlotte (Johansson), meanwhile, is pretty much abandoned in the same hotel while her photographer husband of two years (Giovanni Ribisi) goes off on "glamorous" shoots (starlets, rock boys). He's not a bad guy as such – just preoccupied, distracted, neglectful. (Rumour had it that Coppola based

LEFT **Two strangers meet in Tokyo and the world falls in love with Sofia Coppola's dreamlike movie** *Lost In Translation.*

ABOVE **Bill Murray and Johansson "laugh it up" in the May– September platonic romance that captivated audiences.**

> # "There's just something about her; she does that cool wise-ass character so well. She just seems older than she is. There's some innate quality."
>
> Sofia Coppola

ABOVE **Sofia Coppola's "cool, wise-ass" muse displaying those much-discussed, enigmatic onscreen qualities.**

RIGHT **The moving denouement of *Lost In Translation* – will we ever know what their parting words were?**

him on her husband at the time, the fashionable director Spike Jonze of *Being John Malkovich* [1999] fame. Of course, she scotched these rumours.)

Bob and Charlotte, who has a philosophy degree and has dabbled unsatisfactorily in photography and writing, break the ice in the hotel bar – neither can sleep. An unconventional friendship develops. They hit the town, meet characters, sing wonderfully bad karaoke (for her, The Pretenders' "Brass in Pocket", for him, a mournful take on Roxy Music's "More Than This"). They talk lots, realizing that

at any age, certain questions remain valid, certain puzzles can't be solved. They become very close, for a moment, an air-lock from the everyday. Each realizes it won't physically lead to anything. They're grateful for a brief platonic bond, a refreshment of their awareness of the possible. For the first time in too long, they're actually inspired.

Bob: "Can you keep a secret? I'm trying to organize a prison break. We have to get out of this bar, then this hotel, then the country. Are you in or out?"
Charlotte: "I'm in."

And that's it. No big explosions, no major palavers. As it hums its gentle tune, *Lost in Translation* makes lovely little observations, both comic and poignant, about loneliness and learning, commitment and yearning. Bob and Charlotte's ennui

(and subsequent energy) is portrayed via exquisite miniatures. Murray's scenes prior to their meeting are acutely funny, even if they're basically portrayals of a man dancing with self-loathing. Countered against a bimbo rising starlet (well played by Anna Faris, who denied reports she was channelling Cameron Diaz), he's a sitting, slouching symbol of celebrity unhappiness. He's seen through the shallow, but can no longer find the deep. The way he shifts away from a bunch of fans who are telling him he's great is Murray at his most long-suffering.

The film's other big star is Tokyo, shot brilliantly (and also, conversely, bleakly) by Lance Acord. Cultural divides are mocked, but with affection (the hospital waiting room scene is a joy). You feel transported by the mood as much as by the place: it's dislocated, yet accurately so. It's a film of melancholy grace and charm, low on sentimentality and thus all the more affecting and plausible.

Magical to look at for scenes such as the genuinely breathtaking one where Johansson and a crowd of umbrella-carriers teem through pouring rain in front of mile-high neon dinosaurs, yet truly soulful, it seems, as *Uncut* magazine suggested, "both classically timeless and very much of its time". As the camera stays with Bob's limo as it leaves Tokyo, you leave with it, leaving the film, and feeling a sense of something like loss, something like there's a new chapter ahead.

"Everyone wants to be found," ran the trailers. Many of us had perhaps thought this particular Coppola, what with her legendary father and fast-rising brother, and being married to Jonze and all, was a flash in the pan: a media-friendly story, a mere style and who-you-know nepotism thing. We were wrong. This was fascinated and fascinating, bewildered and smart, sarcastic but never smug. "Sometimes you have to go halfway around the world to come full circle."

Let's get lost.

Charlotte: "I just don't know what I'm supposed to be."
Bob: "You'll figure that out."

The bittersweet bubble of this study of cultural and individual dislocation became a *cause cèlèbre*. Coppola, spoiled but also spoofed as the daughter of privilege (she'd been to Japan with her father several times), buried all memory of her disastrous acting turn in *The Godfather: Part III* (1990). The movie was shot in just 27 days, sometimes guerrilla-style, for a four-million-dollar-budget; Daddy had suggested shooting on futuristic high-definition video but Sofia plumped for film because "it felt more romantic". Murray maintains it's the best movie he's been in; Coppola that she wouldn't have made it if he couldn't have participated. His whisky-commercial scenes were doubtless a comment on Coppola Senior's own, made in the 1970s with no less a figure than Akira Kurosawa. There were other in-jokes: Bob and Charlotte, for instance, watch Fellini's *La Dolce Vita* (1960). Famously, that classic ends with an inaudible

RIGHT **Bill Murray, producer Ross Katz, Johansson and Sofia Coppola with their 2004 Golden Globe awards for *Lost in Translation*.**

conversation between a man and a younger woman. Of course, the similarly enigmatic nature of the unheard final words between Murray and Johansson (over 30 years' difference in age between them) in *Lost in Translation* has intrigued film fans ever since.

Bob: "I don't want to leave."
Charlotte: "So don't. Stay here with me. We'll start a jazz band."

"It's altogether remarkable," cooed *Rolling Stone*'s Peter Travers. "Johansson, 18, and striking in diverse films … has matured into an actress of smashing loveliness and subtle grace." In *The Guardian*, Peter Bradshaw raved that, "[It's] more than a breakthrough – it's an insouciant triumph. A terrifically funny, heartbreakingly sad and swooningly romantic movie – very modern and sexy." The plaudits were everywhere, from the *Evening Standard*'s "Hysterically funny" to *Arena*'s "Phenomenal" to *The Daily Telegraph*'s "Magnificent". With lots of exclamation marks.

The opening shot had made audiences keenly aware of the grown-up Scarlett's previously hidden assets. Bluntly put, it's an immodest close-up of her rear, in nothing but salmon-pink knickers. This was Coppola's idea; she was infatuated with an erotic painting by John Kacere and wished to emulate it. Scarlett was reluctant to be so exposed, until the director herself modelled the near-transparent garment to prove this wasn't an "indecent" suggestion. Whatever the aesthetic intentions, the charged moment meant the former child actress was now a fully fledged sex symbol. This was something future directors were not averse to playing on, and Scarlett's image was, whether she liked it or not, redefined.

Among too many award nominations to mention, it won Coppola a Best Screenplay Oscar – something she wouldn't get for good-looking, narratively slack follow-up *Marie Antoinette*. It was even nominated for Best Film and Best Director, and Murray was pipped at the post for Best Actor.

Scarlett, however, cleaned up, despite being overlooked by the Oscars. While still at a tender age, she won a BAFTA for Best Actress in a Leading Role, as well as a Boston Society of Film Critics Award, a Venice Film Festival Award and a San Jordi Award. She was also nominated by the Golden Globes, by MTV (Breakthrough Female Performance) and Teen Choice (Breakout Movie Star).

As she told Daisy Garnett in *Vogue*, "I thought with the BAFTAs I might cancel myself out because I was nominated twice. But … it felt normal. It feels like the award has been 11 years in the making." The acceptance itself was less serene.

"Mostly I was busy worrying about my earring. I'd borrowed these ridiculously big diamond ones. When my mom kissed me to congratulate me, she held me so tightly I thought she'd knocked one of them out, so all I could think was: where's the earring? Is the earring OK?"

As Charlotte visits Tokyo's Shinto shrines and is disturbed that she feels no spiritual reaction, as she listens to a self-help CD called *A Soul's Search*, it's difficult not to feel that the young Johansson is playing elements of herself. Or at least of Coppola and herself combined. That would, of course, be a simplistic reading. Johansson had prepared for the role by living on Hokkaido, in northern Japan, with then-boyfriend Faiz Ahmad. What was beyond doubt was that in *Lost in Translation* we were witnessing that alchemical moment where promise and potential become undeniable star quality. Johansson, everybody agreed, had that elusive something. In a film about searching, she was found. She had *IT*.

Charlotte: "Let's never come here again, because it will never be as much fun."

She wasn't about to go away. Her double whammy of 2003 continued with the visually exquisite *Girl with a Pearl Earring*, for which she won both Golden Globe and BAFTA nominations. She began shooting just ten days after wrapping the Coppola film. Although in truth she had little to do in the way of actual talking in this period romance, it cemented her perceived status as a great screen beauty, comparing her as it did to an icon of art, seen through the eyes of a Dutch master. Less generous observers might

RIGHT **Bringing an air of glamour to the occasion, Johansson picked up a BAFTA for *Lost In Translation* in 2004.**

remark that she over-pouts those sizeable lips so much that at times she resembles a goldfish in a bonnet.

"My character and Colin Firth's don't need each other; we want each other," she commented. "But her inner strength means she can survive anything unscathed."

The luminous adaptation of Tracy Chevalier's novel, a hypothesis, a fantasy, a speculation, had been much delayed. Originally Mike Newell (*Four Weddings and a Funeral* [1994], *Donnie Brasco* [1997]) was to direct, with Kate Hudson and Ralph Fiennes starring. Later, Kirsten

Dunst was slated for the Johansson role. Dunst elected to go with *Spider-Man* (2002), and Scarlett – third choice – bagged a big slice of luck, although both Newell and Fiennes had grown bored with waiting by now. Peter Webber came on board, with only a few TV dramas to his name; until the recent *Hannibal Rising* (2007), he didn't direct another movie. And yet the look of the film – a triumph, perhaps, of style over content – seduced most critics. It looked like a Vermeer painting. It did what it set out to do. *USA Today* called it "mesmerizing", while *Entertainment Weekly* opted for "captivating". "A film of great beauty," said Kenneth Turan in the *LA Times*. James Christopher, in *The Times*, was less effusive: "Brilliantly lit and dressed, but the master and servant romance has the erotic charge of a five-watt light bulb. I don't think there has been a more beautiful period romance that never happens."

Of Scarlett, nonetheless, he noted, "Johansson is a shapely marvel – she barely speaks a word, yet the entire drama is quietly frozen on her face." That face was to dominate the film in a way which Hudson's or Dunst's would have struggled to. "That's acting," said director Webber, admiringly.

The plot imagines the story behind the famous titular portrait: the mystery behind the masterpiece. In mid-seventeenth-century Delft, Johannes Vermeer (played by Colin Firth much as he plays every role he undertakes: moody, glowering yet vulnerable) is a promising, gifted yet financially struggling painter. A young peasant maid working in his house, the illiterate Griet (Johansson) catches his eye. She also catches the lustful eye of Vermeer's wealthy patron Pieter Van Ruijven (Tom Wilkinson), who commissions a portrait of her, believing she'll acquiesce to his sexual cravings. Far from it; passive observer Griet is more drawn to the artist himself, although her primary tryst, more socially suitable for the times, is with a lowly butcher's boy (Cillian Murphy). Griet does "see" and "understand" Vermeer's work, though, and he's smitten enough to produce an historically important work of art. All this must be done behind the back

LEFT **As the "Girl with a Pearl Earring" in Peter Webber's popular 2003 period film.**

ABOVE **Colin Firth and Scarlett burrow beneath the Vermeer in**
Girl with a Pearl Earring.

of his jealous wife, and out of the reach of salacious upstairs-downstairs gossip.

"Beauty inspires obsession" – certainly the camera believes Johansson's bonnet-clad visage is sufficient to inspire and provoke risk-taking. There's a restrained, elegant eroticism: Vermeer's pleas to the 17-year-old girl to "Take off your cap" and "Lick your lips" are bombshells in context. "You looked inside me!" is Griet's steamiest line. Yet the film, partly shot in Luxembourg, lacks drive, and it's telling that its chief award nominations came for art production, design and costumes. The characters are surface ciphers.

At this stage in her career, we could be forgiven for thinking Johansson doesn't smile too much. She does step outside her comfort zone here, and in a tread-softly film (in total nominated for ten BAFTAs, including Best British Film, and three Academy Awards) makes few false moves. Every picture tells a story. She's shrewd enough to allow it to do so. Griet is a variation on the Cinderella fable: a few years later Scarlett would be posing as Cinderella for photographer Annie Liebowitz in a globally huge Walt Disney Parks commercial campaign.

With Webber's film, however, she appreciated the compact scale and aesthetic intent of a very European piece. "It would be hellish to have had the pressure of putting on a Hollywood ending," she said, sagely. Then, with a remark that cunningly both titillated her male fans and laid down her boundaries, she added: "Or of sticking in a random scene where Vermeer sees Griet washing her breasts. I always check in the mirror to make sure nothing is see-through."

Grilled about awards ceremonies, she disingenuously chuckled that she'd be eating Chinese food at home unless invited. Fashion labels were already pressing her to showcase their dresses. It was happening for her now. She'd had to audition for the Griet role, but soon director Webber had come "crawling on his hands and knees to fish me back". She never read the novel, not wanting "anyone else's explanation of how the character was feeling". "You find different chords in every role you play that strike true with you," she maintains. She confessed to bluffing that she knew what she was doing with props such as mops and buckets, hoping "people would just buy it".

She had no false modesty about her British accent. "That's actually a strong point for me," she told AboutFilm. website "I'm good with dialect. It's something I've always enjoyed and been pretty fast with. At first it was shaky, but it became second nature after a week or two."

As for Griet being in love with Firth's Vermeer, "It was physically heartbreaking. I was longing for this genius."

Johansson was a dead-ringer for the girl with a pearl earring, a work of art made flesh made celluloid. With this role arriving after *Lost in Translation*, and contrasting cleverly, she now enjoyed a growing army of fans and admirers. "You really feel her heart pumping," reckoned *Heat* magazine. She was A-list, or close. Offers poured in. Oddly, she now embarked on some distinctly dodgy career decisions, even though her name was so white-hot that she easily bounced back, bigger than ever.

7 "A Face Made for Movies"

Suddenly an It Girl, a cover girl, Johansson's face was everywhere. She was landing major modelling commissions, dating her first celebrity boyfriends (about which, more later). She was even doing her bit on the campaign trail for Democratic presidential candidate John Kerry (as were many rock stars and movie people; Kerry, of course, lost to George W. Bush. The rest was … depressing). Scarlett was everywhere – that is, except for in the very best movies. Having left school, she kissed a few cinematic frogs before finding the right path amid all the yellow-brick roads being thrust at her.

"I don't plan on going any further with formal education," she told an *About Film* interviewer at this time. She was dividing her living arrangements between New York, where she'd been born and raised, and LA (where she had her own place now, closer to the film world's epicentre as well as her mother's management regime). "I've graduated from high school as an honor student. I was supposed to go on a film-direction course this year, but decided not to; it really didn't make much sense to me to go back to school for

LEFT **You're nobody without your very own Gap advertisement. A stylish Scarlett promotes sweaters for the clothing chain in 2002.**

BELOW **Slumming it with Chris Evans and Bryan Greenberg in teen comedy *The Perfect Score*.**

something I'm involved in so much anyway. Other things I want to study, like film history and post-production editing, I can research separately."

Asked if she felt "independent", she replied: "Yes, I'm very independent. I mean, I still need a lot of love and care. But I'm independent, yeah. I can take care of myself."

She reckoned close friends and family kept her going. "I think I'm pretty realistic about things. I'm very focused, so that certainly prevents me from going all over the place. I've always been very focused on my career. That helps. But it's good to have people say, 'Okay, you need a vacation'."

She'd actually shot *The Perfect Score* (2004) in Vancouver before *Lost in Translation* and *Girl with a Pearl Earring*. It's safe to say that this MTV teen caper wasn't in their league. As one British reviewer remarked, "The presence of the famous Scarlett Johansson may be the only reason it's arrived here at all. But she can't do much more than look nice." Directed by Brian Robbins (later executive producer of *Smallville*) and written by Jon Zack (*Shrek the Third* [2007]) and Marc Hyman (*Meet the Fokkers* [2004]), it followed six diverse teenagers who conspire to break into the Scholastic Aptitude Test (SAT) centre and steal the answers. They realize, with much corny blending of moralizing and laughs, that the door to true happiness won't be thrown open by a perfect exam score.

Here's what Scarlett had to say about her involvement:

I flipped through the script – at the time I was considering a few other things – and saw this bunch of high school students. So I figured it was a chance to work with other young actors. It was one of the first scripts I'd read about teenagers where the lingo, situations and relationships between the teenagers were believable … you know, it was more than just a middle-aged man writing what he thought was "cool" … There are some characters you just know you can play well, and Francesca felt easy for me…

"After an hour of meeting her," said director Robbins, "it was a no-brainer – a done deal."

LEFT **The cast of *The Perfect Score* had saucy fun offscreen, but failed to outshine *The Breakfast Club* onscreen.**

Much about the movie encourages the phrase "no-brainer", and this film is curious in the way it makes Johansson mostly just a sex symbol, albeit a by-numbers "tough, feisty" one. The most rebellious among the various irritating teens (who include minor stars like Chris Evans [*Fantastic Four*, 2005] and Erika Christensen [*Traffic*, 2000]), Francesca Curtis is the angry daughter of a wealthy exec. She insults his stream of lady friends (in one especially lame joke, she says to one, "Peace. That's p-i-e-c-e, as in – you are") and dresses in wannabe designer-punk gear that only MTV could consider an anti-fashion statement. While for the most part the movie avoids *American Pie*-style scatological humour, everyone seems obsessed with Francesca's underwear. At least when one guy quips, "Don't worry: it's not like I'm trying to look at your underwear," her reply is "empowered" (well, sort of): "Who says I'm wearing any?" But another scene where two young horny geeks (and the camera) stare up her skirt longingly is embarrassing, and nothing short of exploitative. The director admits as much on his awful dvd commentary. After heavy-breathing "That's a good shot," he gushes, "Scarlett called me into her dressing room to choose between panties with hearts on or with cherries on. Well, someone's gotta do it." As if realizing the big hole he's dug for himself, he quickly reverses to propriety: "She's just got a face that's made for movies. She really does. She's amazingly photogenic." So – judging by this and then the entirely coincidental opening of *Lost in Translation* – were her pants.

Wearing a longish dark red wig, she looks very different again in this role. The "punky" outsider is a standard in such high school flicks, but Scarlett, confident as ever, does what she can with it. She's the "cool" one who berates the geeks, until – of course – falling in love with one. She gets some good lines before everything tumbles into the usual uplifting sentimentality. "You look like a slut," she digs at Christensen's prim girl. Then with deadpan timing: "I like it." In another scene, "I'm here to make new friends. Oh, and for the wine," is her given reason for joining the gang of inept exam-burglars. It's been pointed out that the film's basic premise is also inept: you couldn't steal the SAT answers because there are several different versions. Throughout the film there are jokes concerning what SAT stands for. Sad and tawdry might be a candidate.

Redeeming features? Again, Scarlett's dry delivery of her jokes. When one friend stumbles, she mutters, in her now trademark, husky, give-a-shit tones, "You walk much?" A lesser actress would overstate the quip; she undersells it brilliantly. And asked what she'll do in the future, cynical Francesca drawls, "Oh, I'd run an animal shelter, or I'd just be a mom. Not just a mother, a real mom. One who cared more about the title of 'parent' than the one on her business card." There's a beat. "Or porn."

Given a teary reflective speech, she subverts it with, "'Poor little rich girl' is a bit old, don't you think? It's like the oldest story in the world."

There's another must-see sequence for Scarlett fans. In a dream/fantasy detour, she imagines she's high-kicking martial-arts-style in a frame-for-frame spoof of *The Matrix* (1999; all the rage at the time). Leather-clad, and diligently shot in slo-mo and stop-frame action, she kicks ass with a vigour to put *Charlie's Angels* to shame. Looks like she means it, too. If nothing else, this moment in *The Perfect Score* made a great showreel for her eventual entry into sock-pow blockbuster roles.

Despite criticism which ranged from "possibly the worst film ever" to "at the end I felt like stabbing myself in the eye with a rusty screwdriver", the piece still gained Scarlett a Teen Choice Award nomination for Female Breakout Movie Star, an indication of how hot she was on the back of her other movies. Fate had been kind in ensuring the release of those two class acts before this dubious one. "Wearisome," yawned *The Guardian*. "No match for *The Breakfast Club*," pointed out Derek Malcolm. Next to a photo of Johansson on the same page ran the caustic caption: "Human after all".

"The whole cast would go down to the pool at, like, three in the morning," Scarlett's recalled. "We'd play games that lasted forever – serious Marco Polo. It started to get serious: people were getting wounded!"

"I told them they weren't allowed to sleep with each other," says director Robbins. "Whether they obeyed me or not, who knows? There was a lot of skinny-dipping going on."

"We all had a good time," adds Scarlett. "It's nice to work with other young actors. Not just for what you do off camera – like, having friends to go to the movies with or whatever. That might not seem like such a big deal, but it can be very lonely. Also, having someone else to bounce off: you feel like they're in the same boat as you."

So, while she didn't trouble Ally Sheedy in *The Breakfast Club* as queen of the grumpy teen outsiders here, at least she got to have her cleavage ogled and wear a huge mask resembling a severed, headless neck. SAT stands for "secretly a tease", says Francesca. What, ultimately, becomes of Francesca? The closing voice over tells us: "She sold her first novel. It's about six kids who conspire to steal the SAT answers. If they make a movie of it, I wonder who'll play me? He'd better be hung like a horse."

As throughout *The Perfect Score*, we laughed until we stopped.

The next release of a busy 2004 was a more earnest, quality movie, and one in which Scarlett was very actively involved. Her mother, Melanie, was credited as co-producer, confirming the control she'd taken of Scarlett's professional affairs. *A Love Song for Bobby Long*, directed by Shainee Gabel, won reasonable critical praise, if not a huge audience, despite having to overcome budget problems halfway through the shoot. The story, set in New Orleans, bore echoes of Carson McCullers's *The Heart Is a Lonely Hunter*. A headstrong, jaded teenage loner, Pursy (Scarlett) hears of her estranged jazz-singer mother's death. Returning to New Orleans for the funeral, she finds two friends of her mother's in her childhood home. Bobby Long (John Travolta) is a fading alcoholic and former literature professor; his protégé Lawson (Gabriel Hecht) has been trying (and failing) to write Long's life story, for years. The three are forced to cohabit.

We'll let Scarlett take up the tale. In a 2003 interview, she revealed:

They've been living there for some time, about six or seven years. She's welcome to stay if she'd like to, but this is the way it's going to be. There's these two really gross awful men walking around the house in their underwear.

ABOVE **Shainee Gabel's under-acclaimed Southern drama**
A Love Song for Bobby Long.

So she leaves the house, she's all flustered, and she figures, "What am I going to do?" She doesn't really have any place to go. So she reads *The Heart Is a Lonely Hunter* and decides to come back. It's about the three characters living together, forming this very strange kind of family. The Bobby Long character [Travolta] and Gabriel's character are these Tennessee Williams protagonists: they have these lousy pipe dreams about themselves. She's this beacon of light in the household, and in turn is learning about the mother she never really knew through the people that knew her.

It was indeed a strange, self-deprecating performance by Travolta, jettisoning all vanity. White-haired and bleary-eyed, he's quite convincing, and very likeable. It's a pity that sometimes when we see him "playing" the guitar, he isn't actually touching the strings, but you can't have everything.

What Scarlett understates in her description is the film's heavy-duty literary feel. The two men, drunk or otherwise, trade quotations perpetually: among the titans mentioned are Molière ("We die only once, but for such a long time"), Dylan Thomas, George Sand, T. S. Eliot and Robert Frost ("Happiness makes up in height what it lacks in length"). As the three misfits bond – Pursy develops a yen for Lawson, although he has a girlfriend in the form of Deborah Kara Unger – the youngest is the catalyst who nudges the two

LEFT **John Travolta and Scarlett Johansson dance, in** *A Love Song for Bobby Long*, **perhaps a little less energetically than he used to in his early days.**

RIGHT **"A 20-year-old of vivid talent", according to** *Rolling Stone.*

was cosy and cuddly compared to Nicolas Cage in Mike Figgis's *Leaving Las Vegas* (1995). "A collection of clichés about the Deep South, alcoholism and the literary arts," sniped one critic. "Verbose" and "a long haul" were also tossed in, as was the plain bizarre: "Are we to believe that Pursy, in Scarlett Johansson form, sits around all day eating spoons of peanut butter dipped in m&ms – apparently the definitive white-trash treat?"

Roger Ebert was less sceptical. "It's unusual to find an American movie that takes its time. It's good to act on a simmer sometimes, instead of at a fast boil. It's refreshing to hear literate conversation. These are modest pleasures, but real enough. The movie tries for tragedy and reaches pathos, a foggy melancholy." *The Philadelphia Inquirer* praised "yet another heart-stopping performance by Scarlett Johansson", although *Rolling Stone* rumbled, "Travolta is an elegant mess. So is the movie."

One begins to understand why Scarlett had been so keen to work with people her own age on *The Perfect Score.* Her co-stars in her last four movies had now been Billy Bob Thornton, Bill Murray, Colin Firth and John Travolta – none of whom, for all their talent, were any longer, shall we say, boyish. Sure, she'd always been freakishly mature, but you have to draw a line somewhere…

Bittersweet, the movie didn't sell tickets. For Scarlett though, it paid off. There was another Golden Globe nomination as Best Actress, and this despite the fact that in one scene she walks out of her trailer in cut-off shorts, only in the next scene to emerge, leaving the trailer, in jeans. Continuity, please!

It'd take a genius continuity leap to take us to *The Spongebob Squarepants Movie* (2004), but that's where we're going next. Johansson provided the voice for Princess Mindy, the daughter of Neptune, who assists the animated sponge as he leaves his town of Bikini

drunken defeatists to see themselves more clearly. "She's not a kid," they declare. "She's 18." In fact Johansson was now, as *Rolling Stone* wrote, "a 20-year-old of vivid talent". "She's too gym-toned and poised for the loser character."

With Deep South atmosphere to burn, and appropriate blues and jazz motifs (by arch composer Nathan Larson), this was a well-intentioned, slow-cooking film, a tale of synergy between broken people. "Everyone knows that books are better than life!" Pursy yells at Bobby. "That's why they're books!"

A mixed response ensued from the various elements of the Press. It seemed this cinematic creation didn't go deep and dark enough; in terms of portraits of alcoholism, Travolta

LEFT **With David "The Hoff" Hasselhoff, of** *Baywatch* **and** *Knight Rider* **infamy – Scarlett is a huge fan.**

ABOVE **Scarlett concentrating hard on the** *Spongebob Squarepants* **film voiceover.**

Bottom to thwart a scheme to steal her ocean-ruler dad's crown. Perhaps a weird choice for a movie, the cartoon (conceived initially for kids) had acquired a cult TV audience among inebriated students and slackers. You'll forgive us if we don't overanalyse this one, but suffice it to say Mindy's most memorable line is: "With my mermaid magic, I'll turn you into men!"

Directed and written by Stephen Hillenberg, the film's soundtrack shows how hip the cheeky concept had become: such unlikely artists as Motorhead, The Flaming Lips, Wilco, Avril Lavigne and David Lee Roth contributed eagerly. Alec Baldwin and David Hasselhoff were among those lending voices to characters. Ex-*Baywatch* and

Knight Rider man "The Hoff'"s involvement drew a surprising confession from Scarlett, which perhaps explains the real reason for her signing up to the *Spongebob* project. "I so fancied him when I was young that to see my name on the credits next to his makes me go all girly. He was a hunk back in those days."

That's the sort of damning-with-faint-praise, double-edged compliment of which Oscar Wilde would have been proud. If only faintly.

Her next film, *A Good Woman* (2004), directed by Mike Barker, was a slick reading of a well-oiled Wilde satire. Importantly, it wasn't too earnest. And it was definitely funnier than *The Perfect Score*. Despite the unappetizing reversion

ABOVE **Some thought that Scarlett was outshone by Helen Hunt in *A Good Woman*, the re-titled adaptation of Oscar Wilde's play.**

to its original discarded title, this classy adaptation of Wilde's *Lady Windermere's Fan*, updated to the Amalfi coast in the 1930s, retained the great wordsmith's humour and panache. The plot may to modern audiences have seemed laboured in parts, but in its sharpest spells this was, as *Uncut* put it, "witty, wicked and wise".

Barker, a Brit, had announced his arrival with the underrated *Best Laid Plans* (1999) and *To Kill a King* (2003). Howard Himelstein handled the daunting task of adapting Wilde, while the marketing bods did their best to cheapen the concept. "Seduction, sex, scandal!" shouted the ads. "She's

the talk of the town." In another tag-line used upon release, it was leered that, "Every saint has a past. Every sinner has a future." Oscar would have loved it, right?

However, Johansson and Helen Hunt strove to sparkle like Wilde's most elegant, eloquent epigrams, sinking their teeth into female roles which embraced duplicity and cunning. Newly married couple Meg (Johansson) and Robert Windermere (Mark Umbers) become the target of high-society gossips when the hubby's discovered to be siphoning funds off to Mrs Erlynne (Hunt), an older woman of suspect reputation who's fled New York society. A notorious playboy hits on Meg while wealthy Lord "Tuppy" (the reliable Tom Wilkinson) proposes to Erlynne. On the night of Meg's glamorous twenty-first birthday, farce and pathos collide.

Barker kept it looking good, but with lines like "I've thought very seriously about marriage; that's why I'm still single" and "People are either charming or tedious", he and the cast couldn't go far wrong. Charming, indeed.

Johansson played period decently enough, though there's a sense that she's not at her most engaged. She does enough, but no more. She flirts flickeringly with the raffish Lord Darlington (Stephen Campbell Moore). It's Hunt who takes the honours. Meg is somewhat passive, as illustrated by this example of the way she sets up, rather than delivers, punch lines.

Contessa Luchino: "You mustn't take it personally. Mrs Erlynne is one of those women that attract men like a bee to a flame, eh?"
Meg: "A moth."
Contessa Luchino: "Bee to a moth. Mmm."

During a hectic couple of years movie-making, Scarlett had been cannily observing and thinking about the future. A star client of the William Morris Agency, she spoke of starting her own production company. "Every actor has one already," she muttered. She stopped short of announcing she'd like to hands-on produce herself just yet, but rashly declared she'd be directing soon. "I'll be doing that shortly. I'm just trying to figure out what project. And I can't imagine writing a script and directing it and then forsaking a producer's credit, because I'd want to have a big chunk of power on that end. Especially if I'd written it."

Such a project hasn't yet materialized, but we'll put her hubris down to the overconfidence of youth. Plus the fact that, then as now, she was, as an actress, furiously busy and in demand.

BELOW **Mark Umbers and Scarlett Johansson in a break between filming on the set of** *A Good Woman*.

LIFE

AMERICA'S WEEKEND MAGAZINE

Let It Snow!
Let It Snow!
Let It
Snow!

Getting cozy with
Scarlett Johansson

How to Pick the Perfect Wine ∗ Enchanting Christmas Windows

WEEKEND OF DECEMBER **23** 2005

8 *"No One's Ever Asked for Their Money Back ..."*

Before Scarlett could say "Of course, what I really want to do is direct," *In Good Company* (2004) became a moderate sleeper hit. She, meanwhile, had been keeping her profile high via other means. The girl of the moment, she had taken well-paid modelling assignments for Estée Lauder, Louis Vuitton and Calvin Klein, all during 2004. With L'Oréal (because she was worth it) she became every young female's ideal face, joining such fellow grafters as Penelope Cruz, Halle Berry, Jane Fonda and Julianne Moore. L'Oréal certainly seeks to cover all those demographics – apart from the not conventionally beautiful ones.

Scarlett also found that her beauty was attracting some beasts. Before and after partnering up with Josh Hartnett (we'll come to that in due course), she was linked with men of varying fame, from the infamous, bluntly denied Benicio Del Toro incident to Patrick Wilson and Derek Jeter. Minor rock "star" (it says here) Jack Antonoff of the band Steel Train took her ultimate rejection badly, and is widely assumed to be bitching about her in the lyrics to the songs "Better Love" and "Two O'Clock". It's "not human nature", she said in an unguarded interview, to be monogamous, but in more recent times she has felt the need persistently to state that she is "not promiscuous".

Around this time there was also a fling with moon-eyed actor Jared Leto. A perennial third banana in movies, always looking for that breakthrough role that's never quite come, Leto also has a rock band: his dreadful emo group 30 Seconds to Mars has inexplicably sold a million records Stateside. His film roles include *Fight Club* (1999), *Requiem for a Dream* (2000) and *Alexander* (2004). Recently, he controversially portrayed John Lennon's killer Mark Chapman in *Chapter 27* (2007), piling on the pounds to do so, however, youthful indiscretions could not derail Scarlett's momentum.

LEFT **You know you've made it when you get your own *Life* magazine cover: Scarlett appears on the Christmas 2005 issue.**

RIGHT **At a Tony Awards after-party, New York, 2004.**

OVER PAGE **Great old-school glamour for a Louis Vuitton commercial.**

"This year [2004] I went to The Tony Awards. I wanted to look like Jean Harlow, so I had Calvin Klein design a dress." Scarlett was big enough to have Calvin Klein on speed-dial.

The Harlow look worked a treat, nurturing frequent comparisons to the Hollywood vamps of the golden age.

But she needed another hit, and although *In Good Company* wasn't a monster, it took a respectable $45 million at the US box office alone, reassuring – at least for now – those who suspected she might be a one-hit (*Lost in Translation* [2003]) wonder. Described by the *Daily Mirror* as "a romantic comedy with real heart", this was in truth quite a subtle, nuanced film, written/directed by Paul Weitz and co-produced with his brother, Chris. It wasn't really a romance, and it wasn't really a comedy (as confirmed by Scarlett's now-obligatory Teen Choice Award for Best Actress in a Drama). The Weitz brothers had a bewildering track record, full of contrasts. They'd made their name with the vulgar farce *American Pie* (1999), then adapted English author Nick Hornby's novel *About a Boy* (2002, turning it into a likeable vehicle for Hugh Grant, whom they also employed in the subsequent *American Dreamz* [2006]). They made the kind of slightly off-centre, hard-to-define films which tended to divide critics, although *In Good Company* was generally warmly received. Dennis Quaid and Topher Grace were the notional and impressive leads, but every scene involving Johansson was hers for the stealing. She duly obliged.

Dan Foreman (the eternally effective Quaid) is 18-year-old Alex (Johansson's) dad. He's head of ad sales at a big magazine, but after a corporate takeover (the real subject of the story) he's demoted through no fault of his own. His new boss Carter (Grace) is half his age, a business-school prodigy who believes in corporate "synergy" and cross-promotions with Krispity Krunch cereals. Dan, from the old school of deals done via handshakes and personal relationships, is frustrated and irked by the cocky kid, but gradually a kind of mentor rapport grows. Carter, dumped by his wife of seven months, takes a shine to Dan's family: his wife (Marg Helgenberger) and two daughters. But it's daughter Alex that falls in love with him. When Dan finds out

that Carter has added personal insult to professional injury, surely no friendship can survive ...?

The unorthodox love affair between Carter and Alex is just about believable, as Johansson and Grace somehow merge their disparate quirks. Ashton Kutcher was originally up for the Carter role; when he had to bail out, his *That '70s Show* co-star was asked to audition as his replacement – *four times*. Grace is a better actor than he's given credit for; perhaps his *Spider-Man 3* (2007) exertions will win him a larger fan base. He and Johansson have some intentionally awkward, blush-inducing scenes.

Alex is a sporty type, a tennis ace. Beating dad Quaid on the court, Scarlett grunts like Monica Seles (that's method!). As she and Carter bond, she says, "I'm not into being 'the jock'. People don't invite me to parties 'cause they think I'm training. There's also a rumour going around that I'm a lesbian." Johansson is in her element delivering such lines deadpan. When Alex goes to college in New York, Carter, catching her reading Chekhov's *Early Short Stories*, elicits the following confession from her: "My creative writing classes are going great. I've always been interested in stories, in escaping into other people's lives. Guess that's 'cause mine always seemed so boring." Naturally we could read much significance into that quote by taking it out of context and applying it to Johansson's own life.

By the time Alex is seducing Carter – taking him to her dorm room, past a sign that reads "Marijuana – because your friends just aren't very funny" – Johannson's turning up the heat, but only in that frosty, distanced way of hers. "I wish you weren't so beautiful," he whimpers.

"I'm not," she states, flatly.

Infatuated, he soon has her picture as his screensaver. Recent statistics have revealed that 65 per cent of the male population actually has Scarlett Johansson's picture as a screensaver. Approximately.

During this prickly scene, Alex breaks the sexual tension (or what passes for it in a Weitz brothers' film) by chuckling, "I was just thinking about how my dad said he'd wire this place with video surveillance."

"Yeah," splutters Carter. "That's hilarious."

Alex's relationship with her dad is also nicely played,

LEFT Scarlett relished playing a character who read Chekhov for fun in Paul Weitz's 2004 film *In Good Company.*

than anyone in my entire life," he says.

"Thank you. Me too."

The film is gauche like that, and all the more disarming for it. A hip soundtrack (The Shins, Iron and Wine, David Byrne) lends it "alternative" cred. As a trivial aside, Scarlett's old friend Colleen Camp, so involved in *An American Rhapsody* (2001; that important building block in Scarlett's career), plays a cameo role.

The film left a warm glow but never gushed, thanks to its chilly satirizing of the corporate mentality. It served Johansson well; Quaid and Grace are admirable actors who drive a story while making their colleagues look good too. Not everybody was unconditionally wooed, however; one online critic remarked, "The luminous Scarlett Johansson has developed some actorly tics: faraway looks and smiles, confusion and curiosity always undercut by wistfulness." He had a point. She was humming some of the same tunes too often. "And yet she does wonders, even with thankless roles ..." Another point, well made. In both *Match Point* and its polar opposite *The Island*, she was to play some very different tunes in 2005, a crucial year for her.

Nola: "Men always seem to wonder. They think I'd be something very special."
Chris: "And are you?"
Nola: "Well, no one's ever asked for their money back."

Match Point, 2005

Despite turning down roles in oddball indie *Thumbsucker* and big-league blockbuster *Mission: Impossible III* (we'll discuss the effect of those decisions shortly), Johansson made two massive movies in 2005. One was massive for the kudos it brought her as a top-level thespian working with one of the all-time legends of filmmaking. And the other was loud, expensive ($126 million in the making) and just plain huge – except when it came to putting backsides on seats.

The first was Woody Allen's *Match Point*. Brooklyn-born Allan Stewart Kingsburg ("Woody") was now in his seventieth

without excess sentimentality. "We made a deal we'd always be honest with each other, remember?" asks Quaid.

"Dad," Alex replies, "I was like five years old when we made that deal."

"Yeah," muses Quaid, "I liked you better then."

Alex and Carter split up with extremely mature civility.

"I just want you to know I enjoyed talking to you more

RIGHT "Scarlett is such a strong actress", declared 70-year-old Woody Allen, signing her up for his first UK-made film.

year. His films had been pre-eminent for nearly four decades. Beginning with broad madcap farces like *Bananas* (1971) and *Love and Death* (1975), he'd dominated the 1970s and '80s, moving into a more serious key while remaining, when appropriate, the king of the self-analytical one-liner. *Annie Hall* (1977), *Manhattan* (1979) and *Stardust Memories* (1980) represent his first golden period, fusing blackly comic and romantic insight. Another hot streak came with dramatic, less jocular movies such as *Hannah and Her Sisters* (1986), *Crimes and Misdemeanors* (1989) and *Husbands and Wives* (1992). In the twenty-first century he'd floundered a little, eking out below-par romps like *Small Time Crooks* (2000) and the confused *Melinda and Melinda* (2004). One constant remained: any actor or actress alive seemed willing to leap without hesitation into a part in a Woody Allen film, whatever the tone.

He'd often stuck with a single female lead for a run of movies, Diane Keaton and Mia Farrow being the obvious examples. Oscar nominations tended to drop into the laps of his cast. Thus, when he cited Scarlett Johansson as his new

> "I can only quote myself from the movie Manhattan. Scarlett is God's answer to Job. God would say, 'I've created a terrifying and horrible universe, but I can also make one of these, so stop complaining'.
>
> Woody Allen

ABOVE **Enjoying a clinch with Jonathan Rhys Meyers in the compelling, but not typically Woody Allen, drama** *Match Point.*

favourite player, it marked a watershed in her career. She was finally deemed to be up there with the most respected actresses in the business, as well as Jennifer Tilly. This role had originally been offered to the very British Kate Winslet, but she dropped out, to "spend more time with her kids". Allen spoke highly of Johansson after working with her, casting her in his next opus, *Scoop*. He raved, "I'm very bullish about *Match Point* and I'm usually not about my films – I usually want to crawl into the ground after I make one. But I'm very bullish about this because Scarlett Johansson is such a strong actress." This from the man who'd once said, "For some reason I started to write from the woman's point of view all the time. Something turned around." For all the Woodster's critics, that something had been a sizeable

career boon to Dianne Wiest, Mira Sorvino, Helena Bonham Carter, Juliette Lewis and countless others. Including, now, the latest hot girl on the block.

Thankfully, Woody didn't give himself a part as Scarlett's love interest. He'd received much criticism in recent years for continuing to cast himself opposite much younger women despite being their grandfathers' age. Controversial events in his personal life, and a much-publicized fall-out with Farrow, had made this trait unpalatable to most viewers.

Match Point was different in many ways to the previous highlights of his *oeuvre*. It went to places he hadn't visited before. It was serious, it was genuinely sexy – and it was set and shot in London. For the man whose name was practically synonymous with New York, this was radical. On a pragmatic level, the BBC had offered funding, and as Allen is never as appreciated or backed in the States as we Brits assume he is, this appealed. But on a poetic level, the milieu brought fresh legs to his work. New contexts added new spice to his philosophical dilemmas. They also brought scepticism: many critics remarked on the tourist-board notion of London displayed by the film (every landmark was shoehorned in, characters zipped past the London Eye to the Tate Modern). Worse, his normally sparkling dialogue was accused of expository clunkiness, as his characters struggled to adapt to the way English people naturally speak English.

Nonetheless, the film garnered more acclaim than any of his work had done in years. "His best film in 15 years" became a standard phrase. It was lapped up, especially by UK audiences, and Allen gained another Oscar nomination for Best Screenplay, despite the grumbling of, for example,

The Observer: "Everyone talks in clumsy, lumbering dialogue that draws unintentional laughter."

As the American character among conniving posh Brits, Scarlett was allowed to speak in her native accent, but even then her performance drew flak: when announcing that she was from Colorado, she pronounced it not like a native Coloradan but like an East Coast American. However, everything else about her role as a troubled *femme fatale* drew rapturous approval. And wolf whistles. It arguably established her as the number-one sex symbol in the entertainment world today. Iconic and sultry in a white dress, she caused men to roll over and humbly (if futilely) offer their bellies for tickling.

The plot – which for Allen was an uncharacteristically tense thriller, full of twists – was heavily *noir*. Chris Wilton (Jonathan Rhys Meyers, star of *Velvet Goldmine* [1998]) is a former tennis pro, working as an instructor. A social climber,

BELOW **"Men always seem to wonder. They think I'd be something special."** *Match Point* **played cleverly on her sex-symbol status.**

he lucks out when befriended by rich boy Tom Hewett (Matthew Goode). Introduced to affluent circles, he charms Tom's sister Chloe (Emily Mortimer). One sighting of Tom's fiancée, American wannabe actress Nola Rice (Johansson), is enough to tempt him to stray from "nice girl" Chloe. Failing to resist temptation, Chris and tragic beauty Nola embark on a passionate affair. They try to juggle their secrets, but something's gotta give, and Chris deliberates over drastic, fatal action …

This is Woody's stab at *Crime and Punishment* (as in Dostoevsky). A study of morals and consequences, it's also a query as to whether fate and destiny are actually overblown words for dumb, random luck. The issue is laid out early:

"The man who said 'I'd rather be lucky than good' saw deeply into life," insists Chris. "People are afraid to face how great a part of life is dependent on luck. It's scary to think that so much is out of one's control."

There is nothing cuddly or sweet about this story; it follows its premise to a bitter conclusion.

The love/lust between Rhys Meyers's Chris and Johansson's Nola – the two outsiders to the moneyed English clan – is depicted as matching the great heated romances of *film noir*; there are modern spins on *Double Indemnity* or *The Postman Always Rings Twice* in its eroticism. Scarlett makes a convincing temptress, but is equally impressive as Nola's vulnerability starts to show between the cracks in her façade. The pair barge past initial

BELOW **In 2006 Scarlett was pipped for a Best Actress Golden Globe by** *The Constant Gardener* **star Rachel Weisz.**

feelings of guilt to jump into bed. "He saw me across the room and homed in on me like a guided missile" is a typical Nola phrase.

"Has anyone ever told you you play an aggressive game?" she flirts.

"Has anyone ever told you you have very sensual lips?" retorts Chris.

"A *very* aggressive game," she smirks.

Scarlett has the lips but also the mix of *sang-froid* and sexiness required to make the part work. "Johansson gives substance and charisma to a potentially two-dimensional character: the Yank sexpot," deemed BBCi's reviewer. "But yes, she is very, very sexy." "She oozes sensuality and insecurity," wrote another, while *Total Film* noted that Chris's "choice" between the two women would not have been hard. "One look at Johansson in a clinging white party dress would make up most guys' minds. She is ace, slowly growing into a role that could come across as slightly bratty, but instead is full of vulnerability." The film, it concluded, was "by turns clunky, compelling and ingenious". *Uncut* found it "heart-poundingly tense and genuinely erotic". For some of us, though, the film's gaucheness, its stilted intensity, was what it made it so affecting and special.

These were not the kind of reviews Allen films usually got: the very vocabulary had changed. London was a factor. Clearly Johansson had turned up the thermostat. In the States the movie was met with a similar blend of shock and awe. "Each and every fascinating character is rotten," wrote Roger Ebert. "Scarlett Johansson's visiting American has been around the block a few times, but like all those poor American girls in Henry James's stories, she is helpless when the Brits go to work on her. She has some good dialogue in the process." And in that process she picked up yet another Golden Globe nomination (for Best Supporting Actress in a Drama), and won a Chicago Film Critics award. (Rachel Weisz beat her to the Golden Globe for her role in *The Constant Gardener*.)

Allen was so impressed he asked Johansson to star in his next project, *Scoop* (2006), which was also set in the UK. Scarlett agreed without hesitation. There was, after all, immense kudos in being Woody Allen's leading lady and muse of choice. It reflected on her generously: she was both "hot" *femme fatale* siren and "cool" art-house favourite of the élite intelligentsia. Best of both worlds.

Scarlett loved London – or at least she did the professionally sensible thing of pretending to:

It's a place of solace. I love London: it's an amazing city. I've met some wonderful people there and I also have some family there. I'm from New York, so I feel very at home in London as it's like a metropolitan breeding ground for culture, art, music and diversity. It's a beautiful city, with history. In Hollywood, it's hard to step outside of the circle once you're in it. But in London I was really moved by how accepted I felt. There was definitely less need to wear my big sunglasses!

On another occasion, however – after *Match Point*'s UK première, no less – she was less enthusiastic, labelling the British press "dumb". After posing for shiny, happy photos and gladly giving interviews, she blew her image at a press conference the following morning. According to *The Independent*, an unguarded microphone picked up a chat between Scarlett and co-star Matthew Goode. "Oh, my God," she said to him. "I didn't see you at all last night. What did you think? I thought the whole thing was awful. None of the British journalists had seen the movie and they were all asking me the dumbest questions." In her defence, red-carpet interviewers are among the most inane and superficial of inquisitors. As for the after-première party, Scarlett showed her youth by yawning, "It was so stiff. I left really early." Her management will have looked out for stray microphones after this *faux pas*.

Around the same time, late 2005, Scarlett betrayed another embarrassing secret, claiming that not just Allen but also John Travolta (her co-star in *A Love Song for Bobby Long* [2004]) were unhealthily obsessed by her love life. "You know what cracks me up? He [Allen] is fascinated with my love life. And John Travolta's even worse: he wants to know everything!"

She'd been more diplomatic in her response to London's grave terrorist bombings of 7 July 2005. On a promo tour

ABOVE **Drowning in passion: *Match Point* was intense, fatalistic and genuinely erotic.**

for a separate project in the USA, Scarlett spoke of being keen to return to the UK (to re-unite with Allen and crew). Although "devastated" by the attacks, she was impressed with the manner in which Londoners had tried to make everyday life in the city go on as normally as possible under the circumstances. "London's a lovely place to be," she declared. "It's as safe as any place. The show must go on and everybody is trucking along. I'm shooting in central London next week, and staying there, and will be for the rest of the film."

This wasn't mere lip service from the starlet, who had been around bombings before:

I was here in New York on September 11 [2001], when it happened, and the unity that people had was amazing. How wonderful the fire department and police were. It's the same in London: they were so fast to act, and that alone can be enough to make you feel like everything will be OK. That threat is everywhere you go nowadays, not just in one place, so it's important not to let it change your life.

Before she could get back to work in the English capital with the inquisitive Allen, however, there was another job lined up. It's hard to work out why she decided not to do *Mission: Impossible III* yet elected to take on *The Island* (2005). Sure, there must have been financial motives, but wasn't *M:I III* also a lucrative proposition? Rumours abound that she was briefly engaged on set for J. J. Abrams's contribution to the *M:I* franchise, but was dropped due to scheduling clashes.

Friskier rumours suggested she'd failed to click with superstar Tom Cruise, and been perturbed by his Scientology talk at a meeting, finding it "weird". These reports were flatly trashed. The less well-known Keri Russell filled the role in question. Needless to say, the film was a big hit. Scarlett's choice of action blockbuster wasn't, as things turned out.

Before we depart for *The Island*, however, it's worth mentioning that she turned down the small-ish (for her) role of Rebecca in Mike Mills's indie hit *Thumbsucker* (2005). Here she was replaced by Kelli Garner. The film concerned a young man (Lou Taylor Pucci) whose failure to relinquish his thumbsucking habit troubles his dysfunctional circle of family and friends. It attracted an eclectic cast (Tilda Swinton, Vincent D'Onofrio, Keanu Reeves, Vince Vaughn) and became a minor cult favourite. It broke no records, but it wouldn't have been a bad move for Scarlett. Having said that, Kelli Garner isn't exactly causing empires to fall just yet.

Coming from a music-video background, Director Mike Mills had been a founding member of an art collective, The Directors Bureau, alongside Johansson allies Sofia Coppola and her husband of the time, Spike Jonze, so she would have enjoyed the experience. In the vein of *Donnie Darko*, *Thumbsucker*, with its hip soundtrack by The Polyphonic Spree and Elliot Smith, was no silly teen-rebel yell (and no *The Perfect Score*). When our boy-man anti-hero is led on for a kinky liaison by Garner-as-Rebecca, she then turns and coldly hisses, "That was just a teenage experiment, that's all." One can imagine Johansson delivering that with relish. Perhaps she'd simply had her fill of playing sexy, stroppy, wiser-than-their-years teenagers. In *Match Point*, make no mistake, she'd played a woman. "Sexually overwhelming," sighed Allen.

In 2005, Mills told me that his story was "... saying: yes, you're broken, but you're broken fine! Let's embrace our brokenness. Life's a bumpy road, but there's great fun in the bumps – enjoy that turbulence!"

Yes, you can picture Johansson tucking into that theme. Mills praised the stars who did take part. "They changed my perspective of humans," he said. "I wanted to show how messy and complicated we all are, and these guys were prepared to dive into the muck with me."

Scarlett, however, was about to dive into another kind of muck. Let's visit *The Island*.

BELOW **Lou Taylor Pucci as 17 year old Justin, trying to break his thumbsucking habit in** *Thumbsucker*.

9 The Craziest Mess

Michael Bay's first film, in 1990, was called *Playboy Video Centerfold: Kerri Kendall*. It termed itself "one woman's erotic imaginative adventure". You can guess the timbre of this auspicious debut. But the director went on to bigger, better things, some would say. Bigger, certainly.

With Jerry Bruckheimer-produced action orgies like *Bad Boys* (1995), *The Rock* (1996), *Armageddon* (1998) and the much-ridiculed *Pearl Harbor* (2001), Bay established himself as the man to go to for unapologetic, loud, over-the-top, explosive fairground-ride blockbusters. They were wilfully unreflective and put the money (lots of it) where you could see it: onscreen. *The Island* was his first movie without Bruckheimer riding side-saddle. It was a "sci-fi action thriller". Or as one US critic put it, "An aggressively derivative sci-fi thriller which then morphs into a noisy, clichéd chase melodrama."

Derivative? Well, only if you consider ripping off bits of *Logan's Run* (1976), *Blade Runner* (1982), *The Matrix* (1999), *Nineteen Eighty-Four* (1984), *Brave New World* (1980), *Minority Report* (2002), *Artificial Intelligence: A.I.* (2001), Kazuo Ishiguro's novel *Never Let Me Go* and cult TV series *The Prisoner*, then sticking them all together in absolutely random order, derivative. Oh, and toss in 1979's little-known *The Clonus Horror*, whose makers sued.

The year: 2019. In a contained sub-utopia, white-track-suited dullards go about their highly regimented business,

LEFT **Don't look down! Scarlett learns the perils of botched big-budget blockbusters in Michael Bay's** *The Island*.

BELOW **Johansson "shooting 'em up" in** *The Island*, 2005.

waiting to win the lottery which means they can go to "the island". In a post-disaster world, the island is the only uncontaminated place left: it's an idyllic paradise, they believe. "You're special. You have a special purpose in life. You have been chosen. The island awaits you." But all is not as it seems: their big brother is duping them. For they are all clones, and the facility is a genetic engineering base, where replacement organs and spare parts are bred for rich sponsors on the outside (which isn't contaminated at all, or at least not in the way they've been told since "birth"). There is no island; just surgery you really don't want, and death. When the two best-looking clones cotton on to the con, they flee. They are Lincoln Six Echo (Ewan McGregor) and Jordan Two Delta (Johansson). Evil mastermind Sean Bean, in charge of sinister forces, is out to get them. Lovable maverick Steve Buscemi (working with Johansson for the first time since *Ghost World* [2001]) tries to help them.

Free from the bubble, the two clones discover all manner of fresh, inspiring things. Like kissing. But mostly they flee. They do bags of fleeing, pursued relentlessly and unforgivingly and very, very, noisily. Things get broken. The plot trips over itself. Lincoln meets his sponsor-cum-maker, who is Scottish and rides bikes and is also Ewan McGregor. Scarlett's Jordan doesn't meet her double, which means she doesn't have to act

> **"** *Jesus must love you! That was the craziest mess I've ever seen! C'mon girl, I know Jesus loves you ...!* **"**
> **Construction worker to Jordan Two Delta:**

quite as dreadfully as Ewan. But she does spot a commercial featuring her double: and get this, it's an actual Scarlett Johansson commercial, for Calvin Klein. Think of the budget Bay saved there! Scarlett brings a lot to the table!

Scarlett is no worse than anyone else in this whole debacle, but that's still pretty grim. Where to start? The way those white tracksuits are clean then dirty then clean again? Several times? The hologram fight between Jordan and Lincoln which is just an excuse for Scarlett to do her ass-kicking routine, only to later hear a speech about how "passive and well-trained" the clones are? The noise in general, which is like three Metallica gigs at once?

"Another victory," as Philip French of *The Observer* wrote, "of special effects over imagination." And that product placement, in shameless quantities: Apple, Reebok, X-Box, Ben & Jerry's, Mack, Michelob, Cadillac … they're all here, in your face. As *The Wire*'s Dave Karlotski had it, "This is what elevates *The Island* from the mundanely bad to the uncommonly evil."

ABOVE **Kissing Ewan McGregor – apparently not a career highpoint, so Johansson undiplomatically let slip later.**

Buscemi gets the best line.
"We're not idiots," pouts Scarlett's Jordan.
"Oh excuse me," cackles Buscemi's McCord,
"Miss I'm-so-smart-I-can't-wait-to-go-to-the-island!"

If the lovers have an almost halfway funny scene, it's when they first kiss and Lincoln gasps, "How come we never did this before?"

"Shut up," mutters Jordan, as tough-deadpan Scarlett is wont to do.

"That tongue thing is amazing!" gushes Lincoln.

Scarlett's unfazed, no-prisoners act wears thin here. Lincoln does something heroic. "Good job," she mumbles distractedly, as if he's just finished looking at her annual accounts. She's struggling throughout: always on the back foot, running to keep up, in over her head and way out of her comfort zone among all the crashes and bangs and wallops. Her face, involuntarily paraphrasing a Radiohead lyric, says, "What the hell am I doing here? I don't belong here."

Despite the usual "failsafe" hype, the movie tanked at the box office, grabbing only around $30 million (a tiny fraction of its budget) all told. The reviews were only a small part of its problems. *Rolling Stone* quipped that "Early buzz indicated that Michael Bay had finally directed an epic that didn't sink to the idiot shallows of *Pearl Harbor* and the rest. Fat chance." Yet even here the charmed Johansson came out relatively unscathed: "A luminous camera subject that even Bay can't sully". She still maintained her hold over male reviewers.

The Guardian, however, was more cutting. "Deafening ... McGregor does that charmless rat-like grin, which is a fair bit less attractive than Scarlett's unvarying inflatable pout." Words like "overkill" and "pointless" featured elsewhere. Justin Chang of Variety.com dared to pan the unpannable: "Faring not so well is Johansson, normally the subtlest of actresses, who in her first major action role has been encouraged to make a shrill, bombastic spectacle of her character's cluelessness ..." Notice how even here, it's somehow spun as not being entirely Scarlett's fault.

"The island is real," reveals Jordan. "It's US!"

Oh, dear.

Perhaps she had an excuse. *Empire* magazine disclosed early on that Scarlett was suffering injuries on set. "Crippling shin-splints" were blamed on her valuable and coveted legs failing to cope with the gruelling physical schedule of loads and loads of running and shouting and reacting to costly detonations. This was not the style of acting she was used to. Was she fit enough?

"It's certainly been more demanding than *Girl with a Pearl Earring*," she said, not erroneously. "I've been coming home with aching muscles, telling myself: 'OK, I've got to start working out.'"

Her hands-on mother had been warning her against overworking. Melanie insisted on time off, assessing that Scarlett was so career-driven that she found it impossible ever to relax. "I'm such a workaholic, but I can't help myself," Scarlett admitted. "My mother keeps saying I should take a vacation, get some rest, even sleep. She thinks there's something wrong with me, that I'll wear myself out. But if I do go on a vacation all I think about is work." Which gives us some insight into her heady, not to say meteoric, rise.

Another news story leaked during filming was more flippant but certainly got attention. Michael Bay reportedly was "horrified" when Scarlett "insisted" on going topless for a love scene with McGregor. (Sit down, boys, it didn't happen.) He told how she'd called him to her trailer and "angrily" refused to wear an "unflattering" black bra in bed. Bay reckons he had to persuade her to cover up as the movie was a PG 13. That he'd anticipated a frank debate as to whether the scene was truly necessary, not one as to how raunchy she could make it. "She says, 'I'm not wearing this cheap-ass black bra, OK? I'm going naked.' I'm like: 'Scarlett, you can't go naked: it's a PG 13'. Classic. She's feisty, I'll say."

Either that or Bay is promotion-canny. He also referred to her as a "pain in the ass to work with", adding, "I mean that in the best way." Scarlett later sighed to *Esquire*, "That story's been twisted and turned. I just wanted a sheet draped over me. Nobody sleeps in bras. Except maybe French women."

Scarlett was equally feisty, if not diplomatic, when critiquing McGregor's kissing technique. "He kissed me like a 16-year-old schoolboy," she moaned. McGregor's wobbly accents took schtick, too. She was critical as well of Bay, and of the movie's producers, once the film had flopped and the dust had settled. In fact a right old rumpus ensued, with everyone playing the blame game with a candour not often witnessed in Hollywood. Usually, everybody gushes about how wonderful it was to work with such wonderful people and learn such wonderfully wonderful things. Not this time.

The producers started it, it seems. Breaking ranks, husband-and-wife producers Walter and Laurie Parkes reacted to the movie's critical mauling and box-office bombing by, astonishingly, blaming the two lead actors, McGregor and Johansson, in a tirade on their website. Scarlett took a hammering. Such lack of tact is largely unheard-of in this arena: you never know who you might have to work with again, whose star will rise. Nonetheless, the Parkeses blamed the actors for the disaster. In this case, poor as the performances were, that was a bit like blaming a parking steward for a football team's heavy defeat. "Listen," moaned the producers, "those are superstars of the future, those two actors, not superstars of the present." Then they really went for the Johansson jugular. "Even lesser television actresses, quite honestly, would have more connection to that audience."

Bay was nobler, falling on his sword. "Everyone from Spielberg to Kubrick has had big flops. You know it's gonna happen one day. It hurts." He was soon in the big (and, of course, noisy and unsubtle) leagues again with *Transformers* (at the time of writing, set to open in 2007).

There had to be a response from the Johansson camp. First to wade in was, of course, "a spokesman". *The New York Post* was told: "This is a clear-cut example of the producers passing the buck and not taking responsibility for their part in making calculated mistakes throughout the film's marketing." The newspaper went on to report that "insiders" were telling them that said producing pair were only seen on the set of the movie three times, and that they were "basically uncontactable" in the weeks just before it opened.

For her part, Johansson, generally said to be startled by the attack – and livid, added to the "spokesman's" statement: "I am proud of my performance and the film." Possibly, she took dignified diplomacy too far there. McGregor was more open. Reeling under criticism from the British press, as if involvement in the *Star Wars* franchise hadn't rattled his indie credibility already, the Scot grimaced:

"It's funny; in Britain I'll get slagged off for doing *The Island*, I know. They'll say, 'What's he doing f***ing off to America doing that shite?' But on the other hand, unless you've done a big American action movie you're not really given any credit."

He had a point: surely part of Johansson's reason to do the film was also to raise her profile and assert her bankability.

There was further feud. Just as tempers were settling, Johansson hinted that she hadn't enjoyed the best of relationships with Bay. In an interview with *The New York Times*, between cooing of her love of her pet Chihuahua and of on-set luvvie gift-giving, she mentioned that McGregor

had given her lots of dog toys, like coats and collars. She added that Bay had "huge" pet dogs, and that: "He needs them. He has a lot of enemies." She declined to elaborate.

She was giving some uncharacteristically unguarded, not to say provocative, statements in interviews as her stock rose. Despite *The Island*, she was a bigger star than ever, thanks to the double-pronged effect of Woody Allen art-house acclaim and botched-blockbuster exposure. In August 2005 she rashly jumped on the let's-kick-Tom-Cruise bandwagon (perhaps that *Mission: Impossible III* meeting had been even worse than rumours murmured). Cruise had been castigated for a comment concerning actress Brooke Shields, who'd spoken of using medication to ease postpartum depression. Cruise reckoned his Scientology beliefs were smarter, and that with them he'd helped people fight drug addiction. After the birth of her daughter, Shields had used the antidepressant Paxil. Tom, in his infinite Scientology wisdom, didn't approve. (He and Shields later made up.) Scarlett made her stance clear, calling him "ignorant". That'll be the part in *Mission: Impossible IV* gone, then. "I think people have their own right to choose whether or not they want to stop taking a drug," she declared. "I can go into a very lengthy conversation with anyone about a woman's right to choose and things like that, but I don't believe in forcing my opinion on people. I do believe that, in particular, children are over-medicated." Ironically, this was one of the major themes of *Thumbsucker*, the movie she hadn't taken part in. "But I've also known people who've taken antidepressants for a couple of months, and it saves them from what could really be a drastic situation. Ruling out something that could legitimately help people seems ignorant."

Perhaps it was the pressure of superstardom, her picture globally ubiquitous, but Johansson appeared to be coming out with confessions and statements designed to court controversy. Previously, with her mother keeping a close eye on her, she'd played the bland professional, cards kept close to her chest. But now, growing up in public and maybe rebelling a little late, she was coming across as contrary, or

even surly. Perhaps she did need that vacation Melanie had been mentioning. Another quote was: "We are supposed to be liberated in America but if our President had his way, we wouldn't be educated about sex at all. Every woman would have six children and we wouldn't be able to have abortions."

In *Cosmopolitan*'s American edition she even spoke enigmatically of a past relationship with a young drug addict. She swore off dating "dangerous" men, after a liaison with a cocaine addict which had turned into a "nightmare". At this time she'd begun seeing long-term boyfriend and heartthrob actor Josh Hartnett, leading man of another Michael Bay spectacle, *Pearl Harbor* (and of Sofia Coppola's debut, *The Virgin Suicides* [1999]), and soon to co-star with Scarlett in *The Black Dahlia* (2006), but she revealed that her nameless ex-lover could never be trusted. She'd always felt "a distant second" to his passion for drugs. "It was horrible," she reflected. "I won't allow myself to get involved with someone like that again because you're never as important as the drug. You can't trust them, you never know where they are, they lie. Every time they blow their nose, you're wondering." She went on, in this candid article, to insist that not all her ex-boyfriends had been such losers. She'd had healthier romantic experiences; she reckoned her old sweetheart from age 14 was still a close friend.

"You go through puberty and feel like there's nobody in the world who's ever going to understand you. Then you meet this person and you connect with them and explore things you've never explored before. You never have that again. So you feel like: 'I'm going to marry you and have your children!'" Ah, puppy love …

The year 2005, then, had been a roller-coaster year, as noisy as *The Island*, as intense as *Match Point*. Scarlett was now one of cinema's biggest names, its brightest hopes. How best to ease into 2006?

By appearing naked alongside peer/friend/rival Keira Knightley on the cover of *Vanity Fair*, of course.

RIGHT **With then-significant-other Josh Hartnett in *The Black Dahlia*, 2006. The movie was based on James Ellroy's novel.**

10

All Over the Place

"*S*tars pose nude!"

"Scarlett Johansson and Keira Knightley bare all!"

The headline-writers were having the sweaty-browed time of their lives.

The truth wasn't as titillating as many may have wished. The cover of *Vanity Fair*'s February 2006 issue – the annual "Hollywood" edition – was done in what design and fashion people tend to consider the best of taste. Glossy, careful, largely androgynous and borrowing its idea of eroticism from perfume commercials, the celebrated photograph of Scarlett and her only serious rival for title of cinema's fastest-rising young starlet, Britain's Keira Knightley, was safely choreographed "controversy".

It made a big splash as the awards season hit its peak time of publicity coups. "From ball gowns to birthday suits" was the pitch. Star photographer Annie Leibovitz ensured a professional job of work was done. But though Scarlett and Keira stripped off gamefully, a third party signed to join the shoot got cold feet (as opposed to cold everything) at the last minute. Twenty-nine-year-old Rachel McAdams, of *The Wedding Crashers* (2005) and other movies, passed on the publicity opportunity once in the studio.

Fashion guru Tom Ford, the magazine's guest editor, stepped in himself to fill the gap, albeit wearing a black suit and white shirt. His egotism aside, the move was inexplicable, his presence detrimental and irrelevant to any aesthetic. He told ABC's *Good Morning America*, "Rachel did want to do it, and then when she was on the set I think she felt uncomfortable; I didn't want to make anybody feel uncomfortable." Clearly he thought that for the rest of us, watching him brazenly nuzzle Knightley's neck was in some way comfortable.

Hollywood stars weren't generally too difficult to persuade to drop their clothes, he added. "A lot of women – actually a couple of men, too – wanted to take their clothes off," he

LEFT **On the way to a Tsunami Benefit Concert in LA at the Avalon Club, February 2005.**

RIGHT **At London's Heathrow Airport; headphones at the ready, passport clutched and en route to meeting Woody Allen.**

said. "These are such beautiful people – beautiful women – and who doesn't want to see a bit of them?"

Angelina Jolie also undressed for the issue, posing in a bathtub. Another shot showed a fully clothed George Clooney as a "director" filming a number of women wearing skin-tone underwear. For that all-important cover shot, Knightley, 20, up for an Oscar for *Pride and Prejudice* (2005), was photographed sitting sideways, with legs and arms carefully positioned. Johansson, one year Knightley's senior, reclined over Ford's leg, slightly more exposed: she has the breasts of a Botticelli and the buttocks of a Rubens. And those lips of a bewildered goldfish.

"They were all too busy to look," she said. "Keira and I were totally naked, and here's this guy on his Blackberry."

As her fame escalated, Scarlett told magazines that a normal day off work involves walking her dog, filling her car's petrol tank, having a sandwich in a café. Key-lime pie and a Diet Coke if she's feeling indulgent. "I only wear heels if I'm going to a première or a party: then I like to look like a lady." Otherwise it's "sneakers or flats".

Her next film release was the second London-set Woody Allen project, although at the time of writing, *Scoop* (2006) has yet to find a UK distributor: a sad indictment of Allen's diminishing commercial appeal. Negative reviews in the States did not help. Scarlett, who'd held high hopes for her now-established collaboration with the creator of *Annie Hall*, was dismayed. In August 2006, the film took $3 million in just over 500 US cinemas, a decent per-theatre average, but it maintained no momentum as likes of the more gung-ho *Miami Vice* (2006) and *Pirates of the Caribbean: Dead Man's Chest* (2006, starring one Keira Knightley) held sway. In contrast to the aftermath of Johansson's ill-fated involvement in *The Island*, no producers were throwing flak at Knightley after the *Pirates* franchise cleaned up.

Despite the relative success of *Match Point*, whispers were intimating that Allen was in trouble again. A planned film in Paris was nixed after budget problems. In interviews the director was pressed into discussing working methods, albeit with customary good humour. He told *The Washington*

Post, "I shoot for ten weeks maximum. Writing a script takes a couple of months – look, this isn't Joyce's *Finnegan's Wake*."

Harsher critics would snap that *Scoop* appeared to have been bashed out in days. *The Washington Post* called it "A feeble, flaccid meander of a movie. It ... sadly demonstrates that he has lost much of his comic timing." *The Toronto Star* piled in: "If only it were funny instead of just passably amusing; if only his movies hadn't declined to such a state of rote self-repetition." Were they any dissenters from the mauling pack? "It's a charmer all the same," reckoned *The Dallas Morning News*. "This time he simply wants to supply us with a good time. And he does." "Worthwhile viewing for Allen's quips," admitted *USA Today*, while *The New York Times* shrugged that it was "not especially funny ... but oddly appealing." Not least to Scarlett's die-hard fans. Like Allen, they believed in her.

Woody Allen himself told me, during a 2005 interview around the release of *Melinda and Melinda*, that good or bad casting can be down to a roll of the dice.

I've been lucky with casting. When I started, I always used the same people: I was going out with Diane [Keaton], and she lived near me. Tony Roberts lived nearby, too. I liked working with friends. Then over the years Diane became a big star, moved to California, she's done a million things ... we're still close, but I've had to break out more. And, you know, when I was going out with Mia Farrow, I did many films with her. Then, recently, numbers of people ... Sometimes I've hired a guy or girl who's been great in three other movies, then I get them and they can't do it, no matter what I say to them. I think: what happened? I don't understand it! Other times I've gambled on someone no one's ever heard of, and they've sailed through it beautifully. You know, there's a certain skill to making a picture, but also luck. Every director sets out to make a good film, but even the greatest make some bad ones. It's never a case of: you're good, so you can just do it every time. You need the breaks.

The breaks, however, just didn't come for *Scoop*, regardless of the fact that Allen had penned it specifically

ABOVE **Shooting *Scoop* with Hugh Jackman and Woody Allen, Scarlett tries to look geeky and bookish.**

for Scarlett. Homing in closely on her performance – and here she was very much the lead, more so than her vampy turn in *Match Point* had been. *The New York Times* had much to say:

She plays the succulent morsel, though this time in the key of screwball rather than noir. Her sweaters are looser, as is her smile. Just barely out of her teens, Ms Johansson has yet to learn how to control either the husk in her voice or that lovely, lush body, which makes for moments both charmingly awkward and just awkward. Her performance is all over the place in *Scoop*, but finally works for a film that is itself all over the place. Mr Allen seems happy to just watch her strut her stuff, and after a while, so are we.

A would-be summery farce-cum-murder-mystery, vaguely in the style of *Manhattan Murder Mystery* (1993), *Scoop* (no relation to the 1938 Evelyn Waugh novel) saw Allen again admiring England's affluent upper crust. Scarlett plays Sondra Pransky, a naïve American journalism student. She travels to England to interview a famous film director three times her age, but winds up in bed with him (a scenario Allen's critics loathed, putting it down to "wish-fulfilment".) And this before the story's got going. Sondra now attends a magic show where she's asked to participate in a disappearing act. The "ghost" of a recently deceased journalist (Ian McShane) speaks to her, giving her a big "scoop". This is that Peter Lyman (Hugh Jackman), son of Lord Lyman, is "the tarot-card killer". Sondra takes up the trail, posing as "Jade Spence", taking weirdo magician Sid (Allen) along as sidekick. Moving among the upper classes, she seeks to unveil whether aristocratic Peter really is guilty, but falls in love with him.

It's as daft as it sounds, but there are redeeming aspects. Allen seems to have realized that he can no longer play the blonde starlet's love interest, and eases into a father-figure role, cracking jokes. The downside of this arrangement is that once the film becomes notionally a love story between Johansson and Jackman, he's a spare part, with no reason to be there. And even next to such random British stalwarts as Paula Wilcox, Meera Syal, Anthony Head and Charles Dance, he does look terribly old and frail. Scarlett, trying hard to play average, even dowdy, instead of sexy, does so by dressing down and sometimes even – gasp! – wearing spectacles. You can see the mic strapped to her waist in shots, and the loopy copycat-killer plot is full of holes. And of course, there's a blatant swimsuit scene.

"I just can't get that vision of you in your swimsuit out of my head," pants Jackman.

"Oh, I'm glad you liked it!" returns Johansson in a splendid line. "It was marked down!" As Sid, Allen gets all the zingers while Scarlett/Sondra has to look a mite spaced-out.

"I was born of Hebrew persuasion, but I converted to narcissism," he says.

She's always setting him up for the punch. "You always see the glass half-empty."

"No, I always see it half-full. Of poison."

Scarlett does dopey-naïve rather well. "I'm a would-be investigative reporter who's fallen in love with the object of her investigation" spells it out. "Jack the Ripper. Is that capitalized?" gives another clue as to this scoop-seeker's abilities. Other lines simply hang in the dead air, blushing.

Todd McCarthy suggested in *Variety* that *Scoop* "will lose Allen much of the critical goodwill and modestly improved box office strength he so recently regained." Well, the British box office hasn't yet had a chance to find out. "Johansson, playing down her sexiness at times with big round glasses

and unfashionable clothes, seems to be channelling both Woody and an assortment of semi-daffy female characters from his previous pics." *Village Voice* went further: "The nubile's reportorial skills seem limited, to say the least. But she's not beyond a bit of feminine wile … if semi-dimwitted."

So: imagine you're Scarlett Johansson. You're 21 years old and your movie career is going great. You're everybody's darling. Your wildest dream comes true: Woody Allen picks you as his new muse. He even writes a screenplay as a vehicle especially for you.

It bombs. You're described as "dimwitted".

You'd be disappointed, right? On top of this, your effort to show you can do big-league blockbuster (*The Island*) has sunk like a sleepy rock.

Which fork in the road to take: arty or safe? How about arty but with a decent budget? Can't go wrong, huh?

"You don't know what's going on behind those eyes," Brian De Palma says of Scarlett. "She's on some wavelength that you don't have a clue about".

The Black Dahlia (2006) was much anticipated, the team behind it mouth-wateringly maverick. But it was not a triumph. Look up words like "muddled", "patchy", or "botched" in the dictionary, and it's there. Flashes of genius, sure, as you'd expect from director De Palma, but long spells of listlessness.

Set in 1940s Los Angeles, the film was based on the first book (his seventh novel) in revered *noir* author James Ellroy's *LA Quartet*. Another of the quartet, *LA Confidential* (1997), had been made into a winning Curtis Hanson film, starring Russell Crowe, Guy Pearce, Kim Basinger and Kevin Spacey. It got the tone and atmosphere just right. This book had been optioned in 1986, and it took 20 years to bring it to the screen, as various name directors, including David Fincher of *Fight Club* and *Seven* fame, pondered it, then shook their heads and reluctantly deemed it "unfilmable".

Ellroy's story was rooted in truth, and in the tale of a notorious murder that had taken place in January 1947. An aspiring 22-year-old Hollywood starlet, Elizabeth "Betty" Short was discovered brutally killed in a vacant lot in downtown LA The details were grisly and diabolical: she was naked, cut in half at the waist, her organs removed, her blood drained from her body. Her mouth had been slit ear-to-ear in a hideous "grin". The media reacted with a typical mixture of horror and relish: her demise, by a twisted logic, became a symbolic cautionary tale to all young women who pursued their Tinseltown dreams. The case was convoluted, the police investigation a maze of false confessions and accusations. The victim was dubbed by the Press "the black dahlia" (after the contemporary *noir* film *The Blue Dahlia* [1946]). For Ellroy, the story held a peculiar fascination: his own mother had been strangled in 1958, and he sought to exorcize demons of his own by probing this still-unsolved case.

On paper, De Palma was an ideal director for the project. He was noted for his onscreen excess and flair for sexual and violent imagery, yet his best films delved into dark places with real authority and packed a visual and emotional punch. He'd made controversial, challenging pieces like *Carrie* (1976),

Dressed to Kill (1980), *Scarface* (1983), *Body Double* (1984) and *Carlito's Way* (1993), as well as showing he could drive a more conservative, slick hit with *The Untouchables* (1987) and *Mission: Impossible* (1996). On the downside, his most recent releases, like *Mission to Mars* (2000) and *Femme Fatale* (2002), had nosedived. Yet he knew his crime dramas, and took to screenwriter Josh Friedman's script (Friedman had just written the Spielberg/Cruise hit *War of the Worlds* [2005]) with vigour. Most critics agreed: this was made for De Palma. But in the end it felt compromised, a film unsure of its own aims and nature. The fact that the case was unsolved didn't help the narrative dynamic. It lacked closure, catharsis.

Around the tragedy of Betty Short (played by Mia Kirshner), themes of lust, rivalry and corruption jostle.

BELOW **Getting physical with Hartnett in *The Black Dahlia*: prudish critics labelled the lusty scene "distracting" …**

LEFT **Hartnett again ruins the daydreams of teenage boys everywhere by nuzzling up to Scarlett in *The Black Dahlia*.**

RIGHT **With *Black Dahlia* co-star and double Oscar-winner Hilary Swank after the 2005 Academy Awards.**

Politicians manipulate cops, gangsters fund sleazy filmmakers. The film's two nominal leads are two detectives, ex-boxers, played by Josh Hartnett and Aaron Eckhart (the latter came in for a defecting Mark Wahlberg). Lee Blanchard (Eckhart) and Dwight "Bucky" Bleichert (Hartnett) are held up as poster boys by the force, but their first homicide case is, unfortunately, this one. They're sucked into the atmosphere of Short's death, into the strange underworld she inhabited. The case obsesses them.

Lee's increasing frustration threatens his relationship with foxy blonde girlfriend Kay Lake (and yes, this is where Johansson comes in). Soon she's batting her eyelids at Bucky, who in turn is torn between her and Hilary Swank's enigmatic Madeleine, whose rich family (especially nut-job mother Ramona, played by Fiona Shaw) may offer clues to solving the mystery. And Kay has dark secrets in the past herself.

Everything wound up dream-scaped rather narcotically by De Palma, which meant it was never the steady, engrossing, by-the-book thriller in the *LA Confidential* mould that may have been conceived. As throughout his bizarrely diverse portfolio, De Palma layered his own cinematic fantasies and vivid nightmares onto the sinister tale, raising more

questions than answers. Maybe it'd been pitched as another *Scarface* or *The Untouchables*, but this hazy auteurism was closer in feel to David Lynch's *Mulholland Drive* (2001) or even Robert Rodriguez' *Sin City* (2005). The actors adopted B-movie mannerisms; the style was luxurious. It frustrated many (with its tricks and red herrings), although if you liked movies emanating from that stoned, weird, erotic state which De Palma inhabits almost as well as Lynch, you could be seduced. Some scenes lingered hauntingly. The fiery romances were tangled and teasing.

But most agreed that De Palma, while cooking up breathtaking camera flourishes and white-hot individual moments, lost sight of narrative – and of Ellroy's vital tempos. Still, as Hartnett and Eckhart feuded over temptress Johansson, the director's trademarks – transgressive sexual proclivities, neurotic *noir* steaminess, visual pirouettes – all smouldered in the film.

The fantasy of a truly spectacular movie had, however, been greater than the reality. There was surely so much more one could have achieved with a subject as ripe as the dark side of Hollywood. Its one Oscar nomination was for cinematography. It opened the Venice Film Festival amid much hoo-hah, and was nominated for the Golden Lion. Scarlett flew in to promote the screening (no doubt recalling her previous Best Actress win here for *Lost in Translation*). But it stiffed at the box office in September 2006. "It veers too far into the realms of pastiche," reckoned BBCi.

Some asides: pop singer Gwen Stefani had been considered for Scarlett's role; Bond girl Eva Green had been offered Swank's. De Palma had characteristically put much thought into his choice of female leads. Kirshner was "stunning", he said, Swank was "a classic spider woman". He'd decided he needed a young woman with a "world-weary" look in her eye for Kay Lake. Having met Johansson years before when she was beginning to make her name

in *The Horse Whisperer* (1998), he'd been taken by her presence: even as a kid she'd made a big impression on him. He said he'd always thought he'd work with her one day.

The Black Dahlia's producer, Art Linson (*The Untouchables*, *Fight Club*), called her an echo of a bygone era and "an old soul". "There's something that's a visual throwback about her. She has that look that pulls you right back in time." Cinematographer Vilmos Zsigmond played up this aspect: there are moments where she resembles the great wicked women of *film noir*'s heyday.

Said Scarlett herself, "When I read Josh's script, I connected with the type of passion you find in Kay. She is this painfully lonesome, woefully romantic woman who just wants to be kept safe from harm. She never knew she'd find in Bucky the opposite of what she sees in her boyfriend Lee."

The costumes were vital to the period feel. Designer Jenny Beavan gathered clothes from across the globe for Johansson, Kirshner and Swank. The women of the time, she said, "defined glamour". "Even when their lipstick was smeared." Swank laughed, "I felt as glamorous as Judy Garland or Rita Hayworth." De Palma swooned, "The three are dressed to the nines and made up to be as seductive as possible. They're dressed and photograph beautifully. You're defenceless against them."

Scarlett enjoyed Kay's wardrobe, her pearls and antique hairpins, her short-sleeve sweater sets. "How can you not feel a sexy dish in that?" she beamed. Yet the truth was Scarlett didn't have as much to do in *The Black Dahlia* as hype may have suggested. Sure, she looked the *femme fatale* part, but the role was underwritten; amid a litany of eccentric circus-show freaks, her character was sexy but bland. Her most incisive line, speaking to Bucky of her rival, was, "She looks like that dead girl! How sick are you?" Reviews nonetheless focused on her more than was strictly necessary – perhaps because Hartnett is always so crushingly devoid of charisma.

RIGHT **In Venice with veteran director Brian De Palma and Mia Kirshner for *The Black Dahlia's* gala opening.**

LEFT **Many thought Canadian actress Mia Kirshner stole the movie as the doomed, titular "Black Dahlia".**

"Scarlett, aah Scarlett," sighed *Total Film*. "Were she a contract girl from the MGM and Warner Brothers glory days, she'd have to be nicknamed The Pout, for that bristling sex appeal. But then that would be a disservice to the multiple layers of softer sexuality she also brings to the role. Her allure is undimmed."

In *The Guardian*, Peter Bradshaw commented on "some gobsmackingly redundant thesping", before scoffing that: "Hartnett becomes obsessed by the outrageously buxom and full-lipped Johansson, whose job is to run in and out of rooms, frowning or sobbing with concern, sporting a fluffy, clingy sweater and a cigarette holder." Said visual aid drew further ridicule, with *Village Voice* adding, "*Dame du jour* Johansson waves her cigarette holder as though flagging down a ride." *The New York Times* thought Kay Lake "a plush blonde with a throaty laugh and battle scars … Hartnett and Johansson are disastrous", while *Variety*'s Todd McCarthy criticized "lacklustre performances and overripe melodrama", before laying into both halves of the celebrity couple.

For, yes, Johansson and Hartnett were now very much involved personally. Hartnett was here deemed "too blank and expressionless to carry the picture – he offers little nuance or depth", while of Scarlett, McCarthy added, "Although she looks properly in period, Johansson also is weak, evoking little of the requisite vulnerability in a damaged woman who keeps the reasons for her hurt, and her real emotional impulses, deeply submerged."

It's feasible that Josh and Scarlett's real-life relationship was colouring the response of some audiences and critics, even on a subconscious level. There seemed to be resentment rather than celebratory dancing in the streets. Scarlett was openly "spoken for", which clearly ruined the impossible fantasy lives of the planet's over-optimistic males.

The couple had known each other for some time, getting together "officially" in April 2006, while on set. Hartnett had starred as Trip Fontaine in Sofia Coppola's *The Virgin Suicides*, so it could be said there was an artistic bond between the two. He's had a blessed career, repeatedly given plum roles despite the public's unwillingness to embrace him in films ranging from *Pearl Harbor* (2001; perhaps he also bonded with Scarlett over Michael Bay gossip?) and *Black Hawk Down* (2001) to *The Faculty* (1998) and *40 Days and 40 Nights* (2002). One is somehow reminded of one of the most scathing lines in *The Black Dahlia*: "Hollywood will f*** you when no one else will."

As early as August, the day after the Venice première, Scarlett was pushed into being defensive, as a few US critics (imitating prim maiden aunts) claimed her sex scenes with Hartnett were an unnecessary distraction in *The Black Dahlia*. It was hardly the "sizzling, raunchy romp" some suggested; in fact it was tame by De Palma's standards – but the 21-year-old was forced to reply: "Of course it's nice to be considered sexy, as a young woman in my prime. But I try not to think about the sexiness. And I never think about it being distracting from a scene." All summer the media had speculated on the romance. On one hand she was sniped at for being free-spirited, questioning the social convention of monogamy and the trials of "celebrity" pairings.

It's difficult; you have to put a lot of effort into a relationship. And I think it's hard for actors to date each other because they are so damn moody. You're away from people constantly and having a relationship that is strictly by phone, it is miserable. Or if you say to him/her, "Hey, (even though) I am doing a very sexy scene with this very sexy girl/boy, I love you and I'm going to be thinking of you when I'm rolling around in bed with this person!"

And yet on the other hand the media made a meal of cohabitation rumours. The same month, there were reports of a New York love-nest symbolizing their commitment. That ever-trustworthy source known as "a source" told *Star* magazine, "They're discussing moving in together in NYC. They've already started looking at places to buy in SoHo and the West Village." While Johansson's spokesperson denied this, the "friend" insisted that neither Hartnett nor Johansson wanted to be based in LA any longer. Hartnett previously spent his nonworking time in Minnesota, while native New Yorker Johansson still preferred living in her hometown,

which she declared "more private" than LA. Other reports specifically detailed their buying a $6-million loft home in the Tribeca area. It was claimed that Scarlett and her father had been sighted with Hartnett in a nearby coffee shop, studying floor plans of the property. A drooling "insider" told *Life and Style* magazine that the couple had asked for soundproofed bedrooms. "They asked us to change the design to include extra insulation between the bedrooms of the penthouse and the unit next door." The condominium, the story concluded, boasted three bedrooms, two bathrooms and two balconies.

Scarlett had undergone one other globally newsworthy experience that summer. Breaking the habit of a young lifetime, and finally listening to her mother's advice, she'd taken a holiday. After four films in a year, she jetted off to the Caribbean in August (before hitting the ground running with a return to work). "I've been working non-stop," she conceded. "And I think it's time I treated myself to a little vacation. What I'm planning to do is go with a couple of my girlfriends to the Caribbean. I've decided I definitely need it. I have a decent break right now. About six weeks, because I don't start again until September, when we begin shooting *The Other Boleyn Girl*."

She deserved the break. On top of the film work and the high-profile, high-pressure romance with Hartnett (which was to endure for nearly two years), she had – and this is just plain weird – been tentatively cast by Andrew Lloyd Webber in his stage revival of *The Sound of Music*. Coming to her senses, she dropped out (although her eagerness to test her singing abilities was to stay with her), and the viewers of a hit British TV show chose the previously unknown Connie Fisher as replacement. Scarlett also featured in a video for grizzled rock veteran Bob Dylan's song "When The Deal Goes Down", from his *Modern Times* album (2006). Here she looked, as often, mildly amused by some secret personal joke. It's a beguiling trait of hers. Bennett Miller, Oscar-nominated *Capote* director, helmed the shoot.

And then came *The Prestige*. At last, an excellent choice that lived up to the promise of magic.

11 "Are You Watching Closely?"

*T*he appeal to an actor of working with Christopher Nolan on *The Prestige*, released in 2006, was summed up by the chameleon-like Christian Bale.

After *Batman Begins* (2005), I'd hoped to find some high-quality scripts, but I wasn't finding myself surrounded. Then I read *The Prestige*, this very original, unique piece about a rivalry with no limits. Because magicians are involved, you never know what's real and what isn't, which makes for a fantastic thriller. It's so layered, you have to peel it apart. Chris is one of the smartest directors around, and I think my passion for this bowled him over. I've always admired actors who are like shape-shifters, and Chris is that way as a director. Whereas *Batman* was a juggernaut, we were light on our feet here, and very free.

Michael Caine, meanwhile, who knows a thing or two about movie-makers, compared Nolan to Alfred Hitchcock.

Scarlett, too – who in another era might have made a classic "Hitchcock blonde" – had been magnetized by the screenplay. "It was one of the best scripts I'd read," she said. "And I thought it would be great fun to play this vivacious, bohemian character. There's a spiciness to Olivia Wenscombe. I think Chris really homed in on that, and I felt there was a part of me that I could bring to her."

Between episodes of the *Batman* franchise he'd reinvigorated, one imagines that Nolan, possibly Britain's most intriguing filmmaker, was granted *carte blanche*. He'd been interested in adapting Christopher Priest's novel about two feuding Victorian magicians since the week he finished shooting *Memento* (clearly engaged by its probing of issues like identity, *trompe l'oeil*, sleight of hand). With his brother Jonathan, co-scripter of that superb 2001 narrative narcotic starring Guy Pearce, he developed a story which exhibited his avowed love of Orson Welles's alchemy of angles and

LEFT **It's magic time.** *The Prestige* **was undeniably a triumph, even if Scarlett wasn't quite the star.**

RIGHT **Teamed up with Hugh Jackman again for the Chris Nolan film** *The Prestige*, **2006.**

RIGHT Abracadabra! A scantily clad Johansson demonstrates an illusion in *The Prestige*.

perspective. Boasting a heaven-sent cast, *The Prestige* was a heart-pumping thriller and mesmerizing mind-game, during which you didn't dare blink for fear of missing a trick. There hadn't been a tighter, more every-second-counts movie since, well, *Memento*. You immediately wanted to see it again, to fathom where the smoke and mirrors fooled you and where this brilliant director wilfully misdirected you.

The plot, or its bones: in *fin de siècle* Victorian London, Robert Angier (Hugh Jackman) and Alfred Borden (Christian Bale) are up-and-coming illusionists, mentored by sage-like Cutter (Michael Caine). Angier's a flashy, elegant showman, Borden a Cockney tough with more natural talent and, initially, greater keenness to get his hands dirty. When Angier's wife (Piper Perabo) is killed in an on-stage accident, he lays the blame at Borden's door. The rivalry escalates, as does their fame. Soon it's out of control, a battle, with neither baulking at inflicting physical/psychological harm. Glamorous assistant Olivia Wenscombe (Johansson in a relatively subsidiary, decidedly bosomy role) is but a trophy pawn and minor player (they think). Using complex flashback structures, we're shown their diaries as Borden faces trial for Angier's murder. Craving the ultimate trick to better his foe, a tormented Angier had travelled to Colorado to seek out electrical pioneer Nikola Tesla (a poignantly ageing David Bowie, rueful and precise) while both anti-heroes allowed spiralling obsession to wound those closest to them. Who's to emerge the Mozart, who the Salieri?

The intensity is palpable; how it's achieved, less so. Breathtaking fast edits and multiple cut-aways bounce you between various time frames until the truth behind the bells and whistles is (perhaps) revealed. With the powerhouse cast encouraged to play on their cinematic personae (Bale's Batman/Bateman versus Jackman's Wolverine in a Borges universe, anyone? Harry Palmer and Aladdin Sane with added gravitas?), there are never less than a postmodern palmful of levels going on. From its opening line – "Are you watching closely?" – to the final heartbeat, this is Nolan ablaze, questioning every inch of the form's envelope yet keeping you twitching on the seat-edge. Abracadabra, indeed.

This astounding film from a modern master (Sam Mendes had been keen to direct, but the novelist, a fan of *Following* [1998] and *Memento*, preferred Nolan) did well at the box office, receiving great reviews in the States if mixed ones in the UK. There were but a disappointing two Oscar nominations, for art direction and for Wally Pfister's wizard-like cinematography.

Among countless other things, the movie is a twisted, heated love triangle. Scarlett, reunited with *Scoop* co-star Hugh Jackman, emphasized that she could understand her character's attraction to his Angier.

"She's very taken with his passion for what he does. He's one of those men who seems very untouchable, as well, and I think that's quite attractive to a young girl: that brooding, selfish behaviour. But when he betrays her, it really hurts her."

As for Bale's Borden, "Olivia's asked to live among the enemy with him. I think they do come to a level of understanding. But it's Angier she'll really always love ..."

ABOVE **Music legend David Bowie – Scarlett's longtime idol – as Tesla in** *The Prestige*, **where he silenced critics.**

Naturally, she also spoke highly of the director. "He has that rare kind of Old Hollywood quality," she purred. "I can't exactly describe it, but you never want to disappoint him, because you know he'll always hold up his end of the bargain."

Costume designer Joan Bergin, labelling the look "deconstructed Victoriana", spoke of her work with Scarlett being "a pleasure". "It takes a very particular figure to wear Victorian clothes, and Scarlett has the perfect form. Hers are some of my favourite costumes because I tried to design a kind of modern, sexy, foxy interpretation of what a woman in the theatre would wear at that time. It allowed me to be quite inventive."

"Scarlett has", mused Nolan, "an ambiguity … a shielded quality."

The Prestige was "passionate, atmospheric entertainment", reckoned *The LA Times*'s Kenneth Turan, "a magic trick in and of itself". He described Johansson's "lithesome" stage assistant as "nicely pulled back". *The New York Times* noted her "presence" but questioned her English accent. "It's … adequate, though she tends lately (here and in *The Black Dahlia*) to be upstaged by her costumes, which appear to be – inadvertently, I'm sure – cut a size too small." This wasn't ogling; this was justifiable observation. Scarlett's breasts – with assistance from Bergin's costumes – were doing their very best to steal her scenes. "Olivia has a very unconventional wardrobe," she commented, "which is very exciting to me."

Also exciting to her was working with rock legend David Bowie, of whom she'd been a longterm fan. Asked in interviews who her ideal double date would be, she'd routinely answer "David Bowie and Iman". Bowie's acting had been haughtily criticized in the past, but now reviews correctly noticed his "immaculate", "dry, amusing" performance.

If *The Observer* praised "a dazzling piece of work that left me eager to see it again", British reviewers weren't all on-side. "Fantastically boring and self-important," grumbled *The Guardian*. "Johansson plays an unfeasibly sexy magician's assistant with a Cock-er-ney accent that makes her sound like Martine McCutcheon's Canadian cousin." Perhaps Variety. com perceptively hit the nail on the head by calmly stating: "Johansson is good, if risking over-exposure these days."

Esquire magazine's "sexiest woman alive" (a mere ninth-sexiest in *FHM*, mind) had luxuriated in a very high profile for four years now. How much of it was imposed upon her by a slavering media and how much initiated by her "people" (or her own ambitions) is one of those grey areas that can never be fully clarified. Over-exposure was becoming a possibility. Audiences soon grow weary of the over-familiar.

Speaking of the magician's art, Scarlett had said, "It's very secretive and competitive. It's all about the commitment to the illusion, which isn't that different from any kind of entertainer."

Sensibly, a gap of some months was left between this and Scarlett's next released film role. Not that she wasn't still (hyper) active. She'd lent her voice to "Dolores" in four episodes of Seth Green and Matthew Senreich's "twisted" animation series *Robot Chicken* (2005–6). She could frequently be seen charming the remaining hair off David Letterman, Jay Leno and Conan O'Brien, presenting at televised awards shows, and shining on *Saturday Night Live*. And as a fashion spokesperson, a singer … you name it: "Scarlett Johansson" was on its way to becoming a globally respected brand name. Despite the up-and-down box office record of her movies.

Of course, one side-effect of being overly busy can be unwittingly offending or embarrassing people. Which isn't

too smart if they happen to be the mayor of New York City. Especially if he's reaching out to the film community, and especially if you're prone to going on about how much you love your home town. In May 2006, the Press reported that "the stunning actress" had "stood up" the mayor at a press conference. Mike Bloomberg had hosted the event in Manhattan: it was an initiative to showcase the city's plans to offer tax breaks to Hollywood studios in an effort to bring film companies back to the Big Apple for shoots. Bloomberg declared he was thrilled to be standing (such was the plan) "next to a real beauty, Scarlett Johansson". He paused. "Although … she's not here yet."

She didn't show. The Press leapt to the assumption that it was her fault. Yet she ardently insisted there had been a paperwork error, beyond her control. She'd declined the invitation to attend some time before, she told the *New York Daily News*, even adopting the royal "we":

"We were never supposed to be part of the press conference. I'm currently filming *The Nanny Diaries*, and production schedules will always come first."

The Nanny Diaries was shooting in the New York area, but hey, work is work. This brand of work had begun in April 2006, and the film, produced by Harvey and Bob Weinstein, emerged one year later, after audiences had (for the first time since she'd taken off) had a brief breather from Scarlett onscreen. The movie – a chick flick, in essence – determined to ascertain whether she could play comedy in the genre that the likes of Sandra Bullock, Meg Ryan and Drew Barrymore had previously made their own. If successful, it was to open up further new options for her. In the vein of the hit *The Devil Wears Prada* (2006), it took a satirical source book (by Emma McLaughlin and Nicola Kraus) and softened it up for mass consumption while retaining a fair degree of wit. Scarlett drew on her experiences in *Scoop*, where she'd used for inspiration acting tics from Diane Keaton and others.

Here she plays working-class Annie Braddock, recently graduated from New York University, who takes a job as a nanny to a rich, Upper East Side family. Mr and Mrs X (Paul Giamatti and Laura Linney) require somebody to mind their

LEFT **Scarlett shooting** *The Nanny Diaries* **in New York, 2006. The directing team behind** *American Splendor* **were a surprise choice.**

the directors' names; Shari Springer Berman and Robert Pulcini were behind the excellent *American Splendor* [2003]) is given less screen time than we'd like. His character is often "away" in Chicago, having an affair and a break from the dragon-woman.

The original novel had been penned by two former nannies who had aimed at searing, coruscating satire. The movie leans more towards the broad comedy of embarrassment, eschewing the more savage edges of *American Splendor*. Scarlett goes with the (often deliberately farcical) flow, losing her cool in front of her love interest, wiggling her bottom (which is given almost as much screen time as Giamatti), but relishing her sarcastic voice-over, using her husky tones to fine, sneering effect. Yet, much like notional lead Anne Hathaway was a foil to Meryl Streep in *The Devil Wears Prada*, she's a foil to Linney's colourful, controlling neurotic act. The disenchanted Mrs X blows her husband's money by throwing excessive dinner parties, asking Annie to wait on her hand and foot. It's not everyone who'd have the gall to tell Scarlett Johansson to go eat in the bathroom so that her guests don't see her.

Annie's relationship with the object of her crush, the never-quite-there Evans, is intermittently funny, chiefly as she's destined to run into him whenever she's wearing unflattering, preposterous garb for one reason or another. Evans is one of those young actors the studios seems intent on thrusting down our throats at every chance, but by whom the public refuse to be bowled over. Also given a big opportunity in the movie is singer Alicia Keys, taking her second acting role (after her debut *Smokin' Aces*). She plays Annie's best friend Lynette (not featured in the book), who seems to have been shoehorned in just to give Keys some acting practice.

Whereas the novel ended in a downbeat manner, the movie gives Scarlett a big, cathartic finale, where she gets to rant at the X family for their atrocious parenting. Thus our heroine makes the world a better place while undergoing personal learning and transformation, as is *de rigueur* for

four-year-old son, Graver. Annie imagines it'll be short-term while she pursues a career in anthropology, although her mother wants her to be a businesswoman. Yet ensconced in the wealthy couple's house, witnessing the behaviour of the social elite, this life grows appealing. She has to juggle adapting, studying, a romantic subplot with "Harvard hottie" Chris Evans (with whom she'd worked on *The Perfect Score* in 2004), and looking after the pampered brat in her charge. With the obligatory hilarious consequences. Linney has an over-the-top ball as the demanding Mrs X, whose marriage is in big trouble. Giamatti (star of the movie which had made

ABOVE **Once the cameras were off, on-set passions ran high between Scarlett and Chris Evans.**

such heartwarming chick flicks set in the more photogenic districts of Manhattan. At the time of writing it remains to be seen whether the formula presents Scarlett with a major commercial success.

In post-production at this moment is her next release, *The Other Boleyn Girl*. By contrast, this movie, shot in the UK, is a serious drama. Based on Philippa Gregory's historical novel, it finds Johansson playing Mary Boleyn, sister to the equally ambitious (and generally more famous) Anne, who, in the sixteenth century, married King Henry VIII, who himself wed six times. This story examines the rivalry between the two siblings, as Mary, too, set her eye on the lusty Henry. Added piquancy is given by the fact that Anne is played by Natalie Portman, whose leaving Robert Redford's *The Horse Whisperer* all those years ago gave Scarlett's stellar career its initial blast-off. There's another

cute link to that film, as Scarlett's one-time screen mom Kristin Scott Thomas here plays Lady Elizabeth. Australian actor Eric Bana (*Hulk* [2003], *Munich* [2005]) plays Henry. Scarlett will doubtlessly draw on the experience of *Girl with a Pearl Earring* when donning period costume and fetching linen bonnets.

The film is being produced by BBC Films, which already made a much-praised 2003 TV version, directed by Philippa Lowthorpe. In that, Jared Harris played Henry while Natasha McElhone played Mary and Jodhi May played Anne. Justin Chadwick directs the remake, after receiving much kudos for his TV adaptation of *Bleak House*. And the screenplay this time comes from Peter Morgan, who after triumphs in 2006 with *The Queen* (starring Helen Mirren) and *The Last King of Scotland* (starring Forest Whitaker) is hotter than hot – and obviously inextricably linked with royalty.

Let's hope Scarlett, unlike certain members of the Boleyn family, keeps her head. As ever, she has a hectic schedule ahead of her.

12 *Forthcoming Attractions*

As 2007 finds its feet, Scarlett Johansson is consolidating her position among the contemporary celebrity pantheon. If there is one worry (and this is being whispered louder and louder these days) it's that her glamorous sex-symbol status might outgrow her acting ability. But remember how young she is. She got "promising" out of the way early, getting a head-start on her peers through all those films she made as a teenager, and there's every reason to assume that her range will expand and her career choices improve as she plays to her strengths. At the time of writing, a tantalizing selection of major movie roles is mooted. Nearly all of them list one Melanie Johansson as co-producer, so there is certainly business acumen involved here.

Mary, Queen of Scots, with Scarlett as the Scottish monarch whose strained personal and political relationship with Elizabeth I of England (the subject of many a film herself) brings angst both intimate and national, is in pre-production. It's scripted by Jimmy McGovern, highly respected Liverpudlian author behind the *Cracker* TV series and hit-and-miss movies like *Heart* (1997) and *Priest* (1994). And continuing the period-garb fetish, *Napoleon and Betsy*

LEFT **That Golden Globes gag you're just dying to make? Scarlett at the January 2006 after-party at Trader Vic's, Beverly Hills.**

RIGHT **Rumours abounded of a romance with Justin Timberlake after Scarlett appeared in his steamy "What Goes Around" video.**

> "Whose life would I like to step into for the day? The president's. I could probably get some things done in the Oval Office."
>
> **Scarlett Johansson**

119

is said to be "probable", with Scarlett "attached". Penned by Benjamin Ross, this focuses on the fallen French emperor's final years on the island of St Helena, where he – according to this tale – falls in love with a much younger English girl. In real life, Betsy was 13. Scarlett being 22, the truth has been massaged. Excitingly, Al Pacino is rumoured to be keen on playing Bonaparte. The combination of Pacino and Johansson couldn't be less than intriguing.

Also a possibility is the gloriously titled *Amazon*, apparently the story of a gladiatrix wreaking vengeance on the army that decimates her homeland. Scarlett does Russell Crowe? From the team behind *Outlander* (Dirk Blackman and Howard McCain), this is the kind of thing which could be wicked gung-ho fun or humiliating noisy hokum. There are, it's true, many who would pay good money to watch Scarlett get into lovingly choreographed scraps while wearing minimalist body armour. Yet the sorry lessons of *Catwoman* (2004) and *Aeon Flux* (2005) must be borne in mind: Halle Berry and Charlize Theron went from Oscar-winners to bad jokes by leaping into ill-considered "super-female" roles. Could Scarlett one day "ugly up", like Theron did in *Monster* (2003), to get those Oscar voters applauding?

More positively, Uma Thurman did herself no harm by kicking ass in *Kill Bill* (2003). And isn't that *Wonder Woman* role said to be still up for grabs? (Scarlett's on record as saying she thought Michelle Pfeiffer, as the *Catwoman* before Berry, was "hot".)

Finally, as things stand, schedules mention the even-better-titled-than-*Amazon* heist thriller *Brilliant*. To be directed by Jon Amiel (*Entrapment* [1999], *Copycat* [1995], *Sommersby* [1993]) and written by Blood Diamond producer Gillian Gorfil, this purports to follow a jewel thief and a conman trying to pull off "the biggest heist in history". Is there any other kind of heist in movies? And surely it has to be "one last big one"? Unconfirmed mutterings propose Joaquin Phoenix or Josh Lucas as Scarlett's co-star, although this project could be some time away yet. The early tag-line is amusing, and highly appropriate to the current state of Scarlett's career: "When you're this good, you can get away with anything."

Her popularity seems to be getting away with a volatile love life. After almost two years' solid cosiness with Hartnett, the gossip pages are now laced with whispers of a dalliance (or more) with self-styled pop stud (and Britney Spears's ex) Justin Timberlake. The singer, after splitting with long-time partner Cameron Diaz, is alleged to now be bringing sexy back to Ms Johansson. One wonders what he could possibly see in the young millionairess recently voted in a US survey as possessing "the best breasts in Hollywood" and the second most kissable lips (after Angelina Jolie).

In Britain (and this says much about Blighty's cultural preferences), she was winner of a Best Bottom poll. "There are plenty of girls with nicer butts!" she protested. "And who work harder for nicer butts." What she added then speaks volumes. "What about my brain? What about my heart? What about my kidneys and my gall-bladder?"

Having appeared in Timberlake's video for the single "What Goes Around Comes Around", she has invited the rumour-mongers to break into sweats. Press reports abounded that she'd acted like a troublesome diva on set. It was alleged that crew members were barred by her bodyguard from eating near her, and that when she was herself barred from smoking she snapped, "How come we have fire dancers here, but I can't smoke?" (A perfectly reasonable point, surely.) Her publicist, Marcel Pariseau, denied these claims to the *New York Daily News*, saying, "Scarlett is always respectful to other people, and never made this statement. Also, she doesn't have a bodyguard." The same video drew Internet feedback such as "worse than *The Island*", "not liking her curly poodle hair" and "the look on her face when her car flips over the flames is priceless".

Meanwhile, it's said that Diaz isn't best-pleased with the younger actress's behaviour, and that Hartnett has been in agonies over the split, trying to cheer himself up by dating such rising starlets as Sienna Miller, then blowing it by comparing them (to their faces) to Scarlett all evening, and waffling on about his lost one's success and talent. (Smart strategy, Josh.)

Scarlett presents at the Grammys with bad-banter colleague Don Henley and a victorious, Bush-baiting Dixie Chick.

As if a fleet of films and a possible affair with pop's hottest male property wasn't enough to stave off ennui, Johansson has been recording her debut album for Rhino Entertainment's Atco Records, due out in 2007. It's to be a collection of covers of Tom Waits songs. Waits is a unique and unconventional singer-songwriter, whose stories of barflies, bohemians and Brecht defy, by their very individuality, easy interpretation by others. The project is a real challenge, especially for a "style icon" who isn't known for releasing records: she will be judged as a vocalist via a very difficult endeavour. You can't knock her courage – and she's to be commended for forsaking the usual young movie-star route of glibly hooking up with a fashionable RnB producer for some costly videos and hip-by-association rap cameos. Rarely can that husky voice have proven more practically useful.

She has sung before, crooning "Summertime" for a non-profit collection, *Unexpected Dreams: Songs from the Stars*, sung by various Hollywood names. But this study of beautiful maladies and intricate melodies – *Scarlett Sings Tom Waits* is the tentative title – will be something else entirely.

Closing the 2007 Grammy Awards ceremony with a Best Record presentation to The Dixie Chicks (who won the category over, among others, Justin Timberlake, looking on from the audience), an uncharacteristically nervous Scarlett attempted scripted banter with one-time Eagles lynchpin Don Henley.

"So: you're making your first record?" he asked.

LEFT **At the Golden Globes after-party, 2006.**

BELOW **Fashion designer Isaac Mizrahi startled Scarlett with his unconventional red-carpet interview technique.**

"Yes," she replied, evidently struggling to remember their spontaneous repartee. "You got any advice for me, Don?"

Don replied, "No," and as this "joke" fell flat as a pancake you could hear pins drop across the West Coast. Her Waits album has to at least do better than that, and may even add to rather than blow her much-discussed cool. She once quipped (or we hope she was quipping) that her favourite song was "Maniac" from 1980s movie *Flashdance*. So she's taken a healthy left turn somewhere.

Scarlett's also cameod in Mark Wahlberg-produced Hollywood satire *Entourage*, and told David Letterman (possibly gilding the lily) that she went to a strip club on her twenty-first birthday and had a lap dance from "a bony Amazonian". The same month she told other reporters she'd actually ordered in burgers, pizza and beer. She's become a heroine to women crusading for more realistic female images in the fashion world: *i.e.* she's not a size zero, and is loved for her "genuine" curves. These famed curves were notoriously manhandled by gay (and inconsiderate) fashion designer Isaac Mizrahi, who fondled her while interviewing her at the Golden Globe Awards. Make up your own "Scarlett's golden globes" gag: thousands of tabloids did.

"I'm curvy," she shrugs. "I'm never going to be five-foot-eleven and 120 pounds. But I feel lucky to have what I've got."

Despite the occasional lapse into Lindsay/Britney/Paris wild-child cliché (her lingerie-clad guest spot with the Pussycat Dolls – the original burlesque troupe as opposed to the pop band – has been swept under the carpet by revisionist fans), she's made a very public statement about sensibly being HIV-tested twice yearly. "One has to be socially aware. It's part of being a decent human being, to be tested for STDs. It's disgusting when people don't. But contrary to popular belief, I'm not promiscuous." She's waged battles against the paparazzi, making news when the car she was in pulled off a stunt of which Michael Bay would have been proud, blocking the street against pursuing photographers. On another occasion, she held up a sign saying, "The person taking this picture is harassing me."

Sadly she spelled "harass" with two "Rs", so the media impact of her protest was diluted by cruel sniggers.

For a glossy Walt Disney Parks ad campaign she posed as Cinderella for Annie Leibovitz. As an indication of how A-list this celebrity gig was, Beyonce Knowles and David Beckham were the other superstars engaged. More worthily, she was chosen by Bono to front his and Bobby Shriver's ethical cosmetics/clothing campaign, Red.

"It's a kind of conscious, charitable consumerism," she said of the project. "People in the public eye are given a voice, so should use it. This has nothing to do with my career; the important thing is to remember there are women and children in Africa who need our help."

She's also now a spokesperson for L'Oréal, and signed a three-year design deal with Reebok. Her "casual urban streetwear" for "the regular person" is, she's said, inspired by Olivia Newton-John's sultry pop classic "Let's Get Physical".

"Nowadays I'm riddled with self-doubt," she confesses to one interviewer in the American edition of *Esquire*, then bursts out laughing. Later she tells him, "Just don't write anything pervy." She has a Chihuahua, Maggie. She tells In *Style* magazine she'd prefer a Porsche to a pick-up truck. She's been reading ("Does this make me sound intellectually annoying?") Dostoevsky's *Crime and Punishment* and Truman Capote's *In Cold Blood* and *Breakfast at Tiffany's*. Perhaps she's a sphinx, with or without a riddle. The theory has been put forward that the sleazy made-up gossip stories which emerge from time to time in the cheaper media do so simply because in the flesh she has an admirably aloof, remote, guarded quality. The tittle-tattle is a kind of wishful thinking, a neo-misogynist desire to belittle, to bring her within kickable range. One female journalist, who'd evidently never encountered the multilayered Scandinavian

LEFT **Scarlett and friend making a spontaneous stand against the paparazzi, just not with great spelling – oops!**

BELOW **Scarlett announces the Reebok deal in New York, 2006. She'll oversee a sportswear line for the company.**

ABOVE **Accepting the Harvard "Hasty Pudding Theatricals" award for Woman Of The Year, February 2007.**

RIGHT **At the 2007 Grammys looking very "identikit Hollywood blonde". Don't lose that individuality, Scarlett!**

demeanour, derided her "bovine acquiescence", albeit based on her screen performances.

Scarlett seems centred enough to survive the turbulence of young fame, although we mustn't make the common mistake of confusing her onscreen calm (she's an experienced professional actor) with her personal life. In mid-February 2007, she collected an award at Harvard University; every year, drama students there grant what they choose to call the Hasty Pudding Award to performers who have made "a lasting and impressive contribution to the world of entertainment". She won Woman of the Year; Ben Stiller was Man of the Year. (The previous year Halle Berry and Richard Gere were so honoured.) She was given the tribute of a fancy-dress parade, and joined in with the students' own show. "This", she laughed, "is as close as I'll get to a Harvard degree." A week later she was voted number ten in Channel Four's Sexiest People Ever poll. That's *ever.* Angelina Jolie

– always her nemesis in such important lists – came top, Elvis Presley second, Marilyn Monroe third.

"I love acting," she says, "because it feels right."

Has she made a "lasting and impressive" contribution? Impressive, yes, but lasting? Quite possibly. *Lost in Translation* will endure, echoing beautifully; *Ghost World*, *The Man Who Wasn't There*, *Match Point* and *The Prestige* deserve to. A handful of others are more than entertaining. Others are no less than entertaining. Scarlett Johansson is, still, so young.

She was once asked which one book she'd take to a desert island. "*How to Survive on a Desert Island*," she deadpans, as she does.

When you're this good, you can get away with anything. Watch closely.

Acknowledgements

The publishers would like to thank the following sources
for their kind permission to reproduce the pictures in this book.

The Advertising Archive Ltd:
62, 76-77

AKG London:
Sam Emerson/20th Century Fox/Album: 30; /Good Machine/Album: 46-47;
/Touchstone Pictures/Album: 32-33, 112-113

Camera Press:
David Dyson: 99; /Fabrizio Maltese: 4

Corbis Images:
Peter Andrews: 111; /Corbis SYGMA: 29; /Lisa Hornak/Reuters: 126; /Paramount Pictures: 63, 64;
/Steve Sands/New York Newswire: 42; /Zack Seckler: 75

Getty Images:
48-49; /Evan Agostini: 8b, 95; /Dave Allocca/Time & Life Pictures: 21, 41; /Bryan Bedder: 116; /Dave
Benett: 59; /Koto Bolofo/Time & Life Pictures: 74; /Vince Bucci: 56-57, 105; /Gareth Cattermole: 13;
/Marion Curtis/Time & Life Pictures: 20, 31; /Sean Gallup: 40; /Scott Gries: 24, 119; /Francois Guillot/AFP:
9; /MJ Kim: 90-91; /Peter Kramer: 125; /David Livingston: 118, 122, 123; /Lawrence Lucier: 18;
/Mark Mainz: 14; /Elliott Marks/AFP: 10; /Marsaili McGrath: 98; /Franco Origlia: 80-81;
/Alberto Pizzoli/AFP: 106-107; /Mirek Towski/Time & Life Pictures: 19; /Kevin Winter: 17, 121

PA Photos:
Kevork Djansezian/AP: 2; /Lionel Hahn/ABACA: 127; /Starmax: 8t; /Starmax/Allaction.co.uk: 7

Photos 12:
Collection Cinema: 11, 43, 52, 53, 54, 55, 60, 61, 67, 68, 69, 71, 79, 82, 83, 86, 87, 88, 89, 92, 103, 108,
110, 114

Picture Desk:
New Line/Kobal Collection: 23; /Touchstone Pictures/Kobal Collection: 37, 38-39

Retna Pictures Ltd.:
Armando Gallo: 34; /HFPA: 84

Rex Features:
28; /Action Press: 6; /Alex Berliner/BEI: 16; /Peter Brooker: 70; /Bill Davila: 117; /Everett
Collection: 26, 35, 45, 50, 72, 73, 96-97, 101, 104; /Henry Lamb/BEI: 124; /Scott Myers: 12;
/Alex Oliveira: 36; /Sipa Press: 15; /Jim Smeal/BEI: 27

Every effort has been made to acknowledge correctly and contact the source and/or copyright holder
of each picture and Carlton Books Limited apologises for any unintentional errors or omissions which
will be corrected in future editions of this book.

The author would like to thank Dominic Wills.

LIFE

AMERICA'S WEEKEND MAGAZINE

Let It Snow!